FIVE MINUTES WITH THE BIBLE AND SCIENCE

WALTER LANG

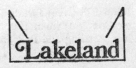

LAKELAND
116 BAKER STREET
LONDON W1M 2BB

First British Edition 1973

These readings were selected from 1971 issues of the
magazine, *Five Minutes with the Bible & Science*,
published by Bible-Science Association, Box 1016,
Caldwell, Idaho 83605.

ISBN 0 551 00416 9

Printed in Great Britain
by Cox & Wyman Ltd.
London, Reading and Fakenham

CONTENTS

1. CREATION AND THE TRINITY
Genesis 1:2 (John 5:39)

Many people like to camp out in the woods and they say that they feel closer to God out in nature, under an open sky among the rocks, hills, and streams than they do in church. They say that they receive more inspiration through nature than through the church.

It is true that one can learn a great deal about God from nature, and can also be inspired. Romans 1:20 tells us that we can learn from nature that there is a God and that He is invisible and powerful.

NO TRINITY IN NATURE

Without the Bible, nature cannot teach us that God is triune, and this knowledge is essential for our salvation. Unless we know that God is three in one, we cannot know that the Father sent His Son to be our Redeemer, nor will we know of our need for the Holy Spirit to create and sustain faith in our hearts. With the Bible we can find the trinity also in nature. Dr. Morris finds the trinity in space, matter, and time. If this is a reference, we could not have found it without the direction of the Bible.

TRINITY IN GENESIS 1

There are clear references to the trinity in the very first chapter of Genesis. In verse one, "Gods" (plural) "created" (singular) the heavens and the earth. Not only is this a majestic God speaking; this is also a reference to the trinity. The Father is referred to in the first verse, the Spirit in the second, and the Son in the third verse, for we learn from John 1:1 that the Word of God is Jesus. In Genesis 1:26 is the statement "Let us make man," and in verse twenty-seven, following the climax of creation, a song uses the word "create" three times, again a reference to the trinity.

NEED FOR THE TRINITY

Verse two uses the words "without form, void, and darkness." "Without form" indicates the need for the Father who placed order into the universe. "Void" indicates the need for the Spirit who brooded on the deep and produced substance. "Darkness" indicates the need for Jesus, the Word, who spoke and there was light and order.

JOHN 5:39

In this reference we are admonished to study the Old Testament to find Jesus. And when we find Jesus, we find the trinity, for He is the second person of the trinity. In finding the trinity in the first chapter of Genesis we are following the injunction of Jesus to let the Bible explain itself, which is the only way to study a book as perfect as the Bible is. By finding the trinity, we find Christ and His salvation also.

REFERENCES:

Studies in the Bible and Science, by Henry Morris, Presbyterian and Reformed Publishing Co., Nutley, N.J. (1966).

2. GOD'S WORD AND CREATION

Genesis 1:3 (Ps. 33:6, 9; 119:89)

In the Biblical creation account we find an emphasis on God's word, for the expression "and God said" is used ten times. God spoke, and there was light, which perhaps placed the magnetic wave pattern into substance, giving it order. God spoke, and the firmament appeared, separating the waters from above from the waters beneath. God spoke, and land and water were separated. God spoke, and trees, grasses and shrubs came out of the ground. God spoke, and the sun, moon, and stars and all that is in space came into existence. God spoke, and birds and fishes and great whales were created. God spoke, and cattle and creeping things came into being. Finally, speaking with Himself, God made man of the dust of the ground.

In Psalm 33:6 we read that God spoke, and it was done; He commanded, and it stood fast. Here we are told that the earth and the heavens were made by the word of God. God's word has tremendous power. It can create complete and mature beings through laws which do not exist today and therefore cannot be studied. God exercised similar power when Christ turned water into wine (John 2) and raised Lazarus from the dead (John 11).

TIME, CHANCE, AND ENVIRONMENT

Today people are trying desperately to find another source for origins. So they turn to time, millions or billions of years, attributing creative powers to it. But time is in itself a creation. If you leave your automobile standing in front of your house for twenty-five years, it will not evolve into a helicopter but it will become so degenerated that it can no longer be driven.

People also turn to chance. Actually there is no such thing as chance, for God controls every detail in our lives.

But if we must talk about chance, God made that too. Chance tends toward disorder rather than order.

Finally, environment and natural selection are used to explain origins. God created environment too, providing for man, animals, and plants to adapt to a variety of environments. These efforts to find another source for origins have failed. The organizing power of God's Word is needed for creation.

THE BIBLE AND SCIENCE

The word of God in the Bible is powerful, more powerful than His word of creation, for He must now recreate us. The same Word of God is needed for science as for salvation, and they should not be separated. Some claim that by using the Bible as a book of science we detract from the objectivity of science or detract from the Bible's spirituality. This is not true. The word of God found in the Bible also created the universe. But the word of God in the Bible is superior to science, for science has been contaminated by sin, while the Bible, through the miracle of divine inspiration, is perfect. If we accept this truth, we will not attempt to find the origin of life in time, chance, or environment. We will rather glorify God for His wonderful creation and His great salvation.

REFERENCES:

Does Inspiration Demand Inerrancy? Stewart Custer, Craig Press, Nutley, N.J. (1968).

Why We Believe the Bible, by George Dehoff, Murfreesboro, Tenn. (1966).

A Defense of Biblical Infallibility, by Clark Pinnock, Presbyterian and Reformed Publishing Co., Nutley, N.J. (1967).

3. LIGHT AND SUN

Genesis 1:3

How can there be light without the sun? When we accept the Biblical account of creation in six days, we are confronted with the fact that the sun, moon, and stars were created on the fourth day. Light, however, was created at the beginning of the first day. As we know of no source of light apart from the sun, we ask how there could be light without the sun.

NEED FOR THE SUN

Some people try to explain this by saying that the sun existed from the beginning but that it was hidden by a cloud cover which was removed on the fourth day. Genesis 1:16 is quite definite in saying that God "made" the sun, and it does not say that the sun, moon, and stars merely "appeared." These elements are referred to as light-holders. The creation account indicates there was light before the creation of the sun; but there is no evidence that the sun existed prior to the fourth day.

We are dependent on the sun for light and life. Without the sun, we are told, there would be enough energy on earth to sustain life for only three days. Harold Clark in a filmstrip points out that if the sun would cease to exist, there could be no life on earth. Also, if the earth were 10 percent nearer the sun, we would be burned up, and if the earth were 10 percent farther away, we would freeze. The earth is delicately balanced in order that we might receive these blessings from the sun.

LIGHT APART FROM THE SUN

That light can exist without the sun is evident from the description of the new heaven in Isaiah 60:19, Revelation 21:33 and 22:5. We are told that in the new heaven God

9

will be the light and there will be no need for the light from the sun or moon.

Man has learned to harness the power of electricity and receive light from a bulb not directly connected to the sun. Fireflies on a summer evening provide another example, poor to be sure, of light apart from the sun.

Light is a great blessing, but it too is contaminated by sin. Perhaps the puzzle in science whether light is a wave motion or jerk motion is due to sin's contamination. If we hold to the wave motion theory that light is part of the magnetic wave pattern which puts order into the universe, we might say that order and light go together. But there can be order apart from the sun.

The creation account records time and time again that God spoke, "and it was so." In preserving the universe today, God no longer operates in that way. His creation laws are no longer in operation for us to study scientifically. Those creation laws could explain how light existed prior to the creation of the sun.

REFERENCES:

Thunder of His Power, first filmstrip in "Evolution and the Bible," by Harold Clark, Review and Herald Publishing Co., Tacoma Park, Md. (1964).

Evolution, Physics and Space, by Wm. Overn. Tape at seminar (1969).

Satan's Modern Trap and God's Creation, by Wm. Overn, Newsletter (Dec. 1969).

4. THE LENGTH OF THE CREATION DAYS

Genesis 1:5 (Gen. 2:4; Num. 7:84; Ps. 90:4; II Pet. 3:8)

On Epiphany, the twelfth day following Christmas, we commemorate the wise men's visit to the manger. There is no problem for counting these as twelve normal days, but many Christians cannot accept the fact that the six creation days were normal days. In an attempt to permit longer periods of time, they sometimes refer to Psalm 90:4 and II Peter 3:8 where it is stated that a thousand years are as one day and one day is as a thousand years. Unless the word "day" in this reference means a normal day, the whole argument of the passage is lost. It wouldn't do to say "a thousand years are with the Lord as a thousand years," for this has no meaning whatever. Removing this passage does not lessen the intensity of the confrontation. The reason is that evolutionists need at least 4,500,000,000 years or they cannot hope to explain origins by means of present laws.

DIFFERENT USES OF THE WORD, *DAY*

In Genesis 1:5 light is spoken of as "day" and darkness as "night," which could be only twelve hours. Genesis 2:4 speaks of the "day" when the Lord made the heavens and earth, which might refer to the six-day period. When the six creation days are mentioned, we maintain these are normal days for these reasons:

(1) The normal meaning of the word *day* is that of a solar day. In Bible interpretation we always follow the normal meaning of a word unless the context demands otherwise.

(2) The expression "evening and morning" is the Hebrew way of saying these were normal days. They began their day with the evening.

(3) The ordinals first, second, etc., are used. Raymond F. Surburg has stated that the word *day* is used at least

1,480 times in the Old Testament, and always when it is used with an ordinal, the meaning is a normal day.

(4) Genesis 1:14 states that the sun, moon, and stars were to be for signs, for seasons, for days, and for years. Obviously, a day here is something less than a year, less than a season. The word cannot possibly mean a thousand years or more.

(5) In Exodus 20:11 and 31:17 instructions are given to the Jews to work six days and to rest on the seventh. Clearly normal days are meant. The passages go on to say that in a similar way God created the world in six days and rested on the seventh. This is a conclusive argument.

(6) Numbers 7:84 describes the twelve representatives from the twelve tribes offering sacrifices on twelve consecutive days and goes on to say "in the day" when all twelve offered the sacrifices, meaning the entire period. This is the same as the reference in Genesis 2:4 stating that "in the day" when God created the heavens and the earth, meaning all six or seven. Moses is the author of both Genesis and Numbers and writes in similar language in both books.

REFERENCES:

Biblical Cosmology and Modern Science, by Henry Morris, Baker Book House, Grand Rapids, Mich. (1970).

Six Creation Days, by A. Williams, Wealthy Street Baptist Church, Grand Rapids, Mich. (1965).

In the Beginning God Created, by Raymond Surburg in "Evolution and Creation," Concordia Publishing House, St. Louis (1958).

5. THE LENGTH OF THE FIRST THREE CREATION DAYS

Genesis 1:5

Today the length of a day is measured by the sun and moon. According to the Biblical creation account, these bodies were not created until the fourth day. What about the first three days? As there was no sun and moon to regulate them, were these first three days the same length as the remaining days?

SCIENCE VERSUS SCRIPTURE

Scientifically, the first three days could not be normal days, for the sun, moon, and stars were not yet created. Today in scientific studies we are limited to these bodies in establishing the length of a day. However, the Bible uses the same expressions for the first three days as for the others—that is the word "day" and "evening and morning" and the ordinals, first, second, and third.

THE EARTH REVOLVES AROUND THE SUN

Possibly we can derive our answer from history. In the Middle Ages most people followed Ptolemy who said the sun revolves around the earth, called a geocentric system. The church of that day also accepted this position and found further proof from Joshua 10:12 where Joshua told the sun to stand still. Galileo was convinced that the earth revolves around the sun and he was nearly excommunicated from the church for his views. Andrew White has used this example to prove that the church has always retarded science. The truth is that the church had taken the current scientific theory (geocentric theory) and interpreted the Bible to fit it. When the scientific theory was replaced, the church was in trouble. Scripture does not change in its clearly revealed teachings, but science does change.

In Darwin's day the church encountered the same problem. Linnaeus had suggested that all species had been fixed during creation week, and this is what Darwin was taught in his seminary training. The Bible does not teach the fixity of species, but those who had interpreted Scripture to mean this were in trouble when science showed that there is variation within species. We must constantly be on our guard to let the Bible speak for itself.

REFERENCES:

History of the Warfare of Science with Theology, by Andrew White, Appleton and Co., New York (1896).

Doctrine of Perfection in the Bible and Science, by Walter Lang, Tape at Seattle seminar (1969) Newsletter (June, 1969).

6. THE PURPOSE OF SPACE RESEARCH
Genesis 1:14-18 (Ps. 104:19; 115:16)

Perhaps nothing has ever received as much worldwide publicity as the U.S. astronauts' first walk on the moon. Yet the reaction of some people was "so what!" They could not see how this would benefit people on earth. And in spite of the vast amount of publicity, there is a growing disinterest in the space program, making it difficult to get appropriations from Congress for space research. Some programs which had been contemplated, such as trips to Venus or Mars, have been cut back. People are beginning to wonder whether the program is worth the enormous expense.

THE SPACE PROGRAM DOES HELP THE EARTH

In an interview with a space scientist, George Morgenthaler of the Martin Company, I was told how space research has benefited our lives on earth. It has aided in weather predictions, in communications, and in the development of new products. Following the interview we asked why these benefits were not more widely advertised. We believe that if people were more fully aware of the benefits of the space program to their daily lives, they would have more genuine interest.

THE CREATION OF SPACE

Some people oppose our nation's space program because of their interpretation of Psalm 115:16, a verse that tells us that the heavens belong to the Lord, but the earth He has given to the children of men. They believe this forbids man to explore space. It is true that space is not made for man to inhabit; neither are the depths of the oceans. To explore either space or the ocean depths, we must take along

15

survival equipment. Exploration is finding vast food resources in the sea.

Examining the creation of sun, moon, and stars as mentioned in Genesis 1:14-18, we find that they were made to give light, to regulate days, seasons, years, and to be signs. In short, they were created for the benefit of earth. This should be our motivation for space exploration—to serve man on earth.

EVOLUTIONARY MOTIVATION

The problem is that the overriding motivation for space exploration has been the attempt to prove evolution. Evolution can't be proved on earth, so the emphasis has been shifted to prove evolution in space. This evolution-minded motivation is a chief reason why the man in the street has lost interest in a otherwise worthwhile and beneficial space program.

This points up the need of using the Bible to direct scientific research. When this is done, we will have a superior science and improved motivation. Christ is our Savior who can help also with providing a superior space program.

REFERENCES:

Witness in the Sky, by Lyon Thoburn, Moody Press, Chicago (1961).

The Apollo and Mariner Findings, by George Mulfinger, Bible-Science Newsletter (Oct. 15, 1969).

7. NO EVOLUTIONARY ORDER IN CREATION
Genesis 1:20

There are people who believe they can harmonize the creation account of Genesis 1 with the theory that the universe is millions or even billions of years old and with an amoeba-to-man development. This is done by assigning long periods of time to each of the creation days and by fitting the order of events into an evolutionary process of development.

DIFFERENT ORDER

The order described in Genesis 1 is quite different from that generally outlined in the amoeba-to-man development. According to evolution, life began in the sea and simple forms evolved into more complex forms. Thus, certain fish forms crawled onto land to evolve into animals and finally into man.

In the Scriptural account man is the climax of creation. And we do not find that the sea forms were first on the creation agenda. Grasses, shrubs and trees were created first and they were formed from the earth, not from water. The heavenly bodies were created after the earth. According to evolution they should have been in existence long before the earth or even water existed. Only on the fifth creation day do the waters bring forth fish and other sea life. Then come the birds, and there does seem to be some connection with water in verse twenty. Then the whales were made, and these are animals living in water. Now the evolutionists have a problem with whales, for they must have them evolving in water, crawling on land to become mammals, and then returning to the sea to undergo changes to enable them to live in water. On the sixth day animals are mentioned before creeping things, while evolutionists begin with insects and creeping creatures before the larger creatures. And then man was created.

DIFFICULTIES OF THEISTIC EVOLUTION

The foregoing paragraph illustrates the difficulty of trying to fit the order of creation as outlined in Genesis into the evolutionary concept suggested in science textbooks. The evolutionary position cannot be reconciled with the Genesis account, and this has led to the popular concept that Genesis 1 is an allegory or a myth; it is not historical, factual, or scientific. This poses another problem: if Genesis 1 is not factual or historical, what about other portions of Scripture? Scripture and evolution are opposites, with the latter leading to paganism which worships the creation rather than the Creator. Evolution does not agree with Genesis 1:31 which describes a state of perfection at the close of creation. Through the sin of Adam and Eve this perfection was lost, but Christ has restored it through His salvation.

REFERENCE:

Creation According to God's Word, by John C. Whitcomb, Reformed Fellowship, Grand Rapids, Mich. (1966).

8. OVERPOPULATION
Genesis 1:28 (Gen. 9:1)

Dr. Henry Morris, often referred to as the dean of creation scientists, has worked out an interesting formula which is included in his book *Biblical Cosmology and Modern Science.* According to this formula, he allows thirty-five years per generation, which is liberal, and an average of four children per family. It would take 1,050 years for the present world population to arrive, he calculates. To achieve the present population in 4,300 years, which is the most conservative estimate of time since the Noachian flood, an average of only 2.5 children per family would be needed, allowing forty-three years per generation. This formula demonstrates that the world cannot be of immense age, and the vain idea that man has been in existence for nearly two million years is utterly absurd.

POPULATION CONTROL

Evolutionists, however, use population figures to push their ideas of population control. They claim the population rate is increasing rapidly and there must be an enforcement of population control, not realizing this whole concept defeats their basic time estimate. They recommend many means, including abortion, to control the population growth because these methods agree with their view that overcrowding will produce an inferior environment and devolution will follow. They hope to control the environment through population control and population control has become a dogma to them.

Environment is everything to an evolutionist and he must have control over it. Thus, old buildings are torn down and new ones built to produce a new environment. Unfortunately they are still plagued with the same problems. If evolutionists can control people by limiting the number of children, they can go on to establish further controls.

OUR LORD'S COMMAND

In contrast to this manipulation of population, is our Lord's command in Genesis 1:28 that Adam and Eve and future parents should be fruitful and multiply and fill the earth. In Matthew 6:31 we read that the Lord will take care of our bodily needs. It is true that we are to plan, to exercise wise judgment, and to work, but it is the Lord who will provide. Murder is not condoned as a means for providing our wants and it is not condoned in restricting offspring.

BUILT-IN CONTROL

E. Norbert Smith, in an article in the *Creation Research Society* (Sept. 1970) reports on experiments which indicate that species tested had been found to possess built-in population controls. Smith believes there was no death in the world before the sin of Adam and Eve, and the animal population had controls other than destruction. This built-in control is called density dependency. It shows there are controls other than death which have been provided by our Lord, and if we follow His commands, He will provide for His children.

REFERENCES:

Biblical Cosmology and Modern Science, by Henry Morris, Baker Book House, Grand Rapids, Michigan (1970).

Population Control, Evidence of a Perfect Creation, by E. Norbert Smith, *C.R.S. Quarterly* (Sept. 1970).

9. POLLUTION OF ENVIRONMENT
Genesis 2:7

In our day there is much concern about pollution of the environment. The Los Angeles area has a real problem with its smog. In years past Pittsburgh and St. Louis have experienced smoke pollution. The use of pesticides such as DDT causes concern. For instance, the area around Clear Lake in northern California has experienced adverse effects upon its wildlife due to the use of hard pesticides. Manufacturers are working to design automobile engines which produce less waste matter, and devices for cutting down on emission are being used. We are concerned with large industries polluting our rivers and large lakes.

EVOLUTIONARY MOTIVATION

Much of this concern about pollution is improperly motivated. Those who believe that one major life form developed from another over immense ages of time must credit the environment for much of this progress. Rather than give God the credit, they say *nature* did this and that. In a sense they substitute environment for God. St. Paul in Romans 1:25 says that when people worship the creature rather than the creator, this is paganism. People are ascribing to environment powers and qualities which only God possesses, even though they cannot demonstrate that environment can produce what they claim for it. Because they believe that environment has produced everything, they are much concerned about pollution of this environment.

SCRIPTURAL MOTIVATION

Christians are also concerned about the environment. In Genesis 2:7 we read that man was formed from the dust of the ground. At one time the chemical value of a human body was figured at less than $1.00; in these days of inflation that has increased about fourfold, but it does indicate that environment is involved in our essence. But this dust of the ground could not give man a mind or soul; that was breathed into his nostrils by the Lord. Christians do not worship the environment although they know how closely it is connected with our creation and maintenance.

In Genesis 1:28 Adam and Eve were given dominion over the earth and its environment. We fail in our duty when we waste or pollute the environment. At one time Palestine was a land "flowing with milk and honey." Before the Jews returned in recent years, it was a barren desert because its environment had been wasted. A Christian has the best motivation for conserving the environment for he knows that it is a gift of God and that he is held responsible for its use. When the environment is polluted, it is not a sin against the environment; it is a sin against God's commandment.

Christ can create a spirit of thankfulness in us and motivate us to conserve and preserve the wonderful environment which He has given us.

10. TO BE A CREATIONIST, MUST ONE BE A CHRISTIAN?

John 3:3

Some people quote Hebrews 11:3, "Through faith we understand that the worlds were framed by the word of God, so that things which are seen were not made of things which do appear." to prove that to be a creationist, one must also be a Christian. They contend that only through faith can we believe that God created the universe using forces different from those which are studied in science. To accept creation means that we must accept God as the basis of all existence. The alternative, which pagan religions and evolutionists propose, is to substitute a creature or creation for the creator. It therefore seems that a requisite for accepting the creation story is to accept God.

ROMANS 1:20

There is another Scripture passage which must be considered, and that is Romans 1:20. Here we are told that the pagan or unbeliever can from his study of nature learn that there is a God, and that He is invisible and powerful. From nature itself he can learn that there is a God with power to create. In Romans 1:18 we are told that some who could find God in the design of nature suppress this truth in unrighteousness. Because they do not want to admit that they have sinned against a holy God, they deny the existence of God and worship some part of the creation, such as time, chance, or environment. While it is possible for a non-Christian to accept creationism, generally this is not the case. As a rule a person must first experience the work of the Holy Spirit convicting him of sin and leading him to accept Christ as his Savior and then to accept God's Word that He created the universe in a period of six days. But there is always the possibility that a scientist or educator, from his study of nature, will be led to conclude that his own existence and that of the universe depends on a God with power to create.

BEING BORN AGAIN

Because it is unlikely that a person will accept the creation account before becoming a Christian, all of us have a mission task. Nicodemus, who might be classified as a scientist or educator of his day, was told that he must be born again to experience the miracle of God's grace working in him. Christian and creation scientists and educators have the specific task of pointing up the benefits of spiritual rebirth and the value of Christ-directed lives and scientific research.

REFERENCE:

Genesis 1:1 and Following by John C. Whitcomb. Essays on tape available from Bible-Science Assn., Caldwell, Idaho (1966).

11. CHRISTIANS MUST OPPOSE EVOLUTION
John 10:27

Greg Bahnsen, a student at Westminister Theological Seminary, is the author of a recently published essay titled "Revelation, Speculation, and Science." In this essay he shows that science must be based on the Bible. Science presupposes an ordered existence, and when scientists propose evolution, they are going beyond the realm of science into an area of speculation where there can be no observation. The claim that things have always been in the past as they are today is circular reasoning. This is not an explanation of the order found in the universe. Either everything is the result of creation by God, or everything evolved through chance. If the latter were true, the order which we find in nature would be impossible. That nature is well regulated is proof of an intelligent God who created and preserves all things. The scientist who accepts evolution claims to follow the facts, but to speak of facts one must speak of order, and this leads to God. There can be no facts if there is no order, and there can be no order if there is no God. It is obvious that the universe could not have arrived at its present state through the operation of present laws, and this leaves only one alternative—it arrived through the operation of laws which we cannot observe and study and which we can learn about only through supernatural revelation. Bahnsen states: "To attempt science apart from God's Word and authority is spiritual suicide for the effort itself and for the scientist who attempts it."

PICTURE OF SHEEP

In the tenth chapter of the Gospel according to John we have the picture of Christians as sheep and Jesus as the Good Shepherd contrasted with the hireling who flees from the wolf. As Jesus was speaking, His enemies asked that He

25

tell them plainly whether He was the Messiah, intending to use His answer against Him. Instead, Jesus presents a picture of sheep, providing the basis for accepting Him as God. Sheep hear the voice of their shepherd, the shepherd recognizes them, and they follow him. The Good Shepherd leads His sheep to eternal life. Sheep are known for going astray without a leader.

With all the boasting of scientists and their self-sufficiency, they are really like sheep. When they rely solely on observation and experimentation, they go astray. As sheep must depend on the leadership of their shepherd, so scientists must learn the same humility. They need to recognize that the very science within which they work demands a God who is superior to nature, one to whom they should listen rather than oppose. They should also realize that this well-ordered nature within which they operate is contaminated by sin and cannot provide the ultimate answers for which they seek.

When scientists learn humility, recognize the need for a God in nature, and listen rather than oppose God's explanation of origins, then Jesus will acknowledge them and bless them. He will bless them with success in research and above all, will grant them the highest blessing, that is, eternal life in glory.

Bahnsen states correctly: "If science (so-called) could actually refute the truths of Scripture, there would be no actual basis for science at all." Success in science today has been made possible by those who have humbly followed their Shepherd and who have learned to listen to supernatural revelation as well as results of their experiments, and who have found the reason for order in nature. They have been acknowledged by Jesus and have followed Him.

SCIENCE AS SHEEP

Possibly this is carrying the picture a bit far. Not only should scientists follow Jesus as humble sheep, but the various science disciplines should also follow the example of sheep. Let us dispel this harsh picture that science does not need God and that it can operate successfully without His direction. As sheep without a shepherd go astray and are destroyed, so science has gone astray and is destroying itself. For achieving its greatest potential, science should humbly follow the direction of the Good Shepherd.

REFERENCE:

"Revelation, Speculation, and Science," by Greg Bahnsen, in *Presbyterian Guardian*, December 1970 and January 1971. Vol. 40, No. 1.

12. IS SCIENCE OPPOSED TO THE CROSS?

I Corinthians 1:20

Paul Zimmerman is a theologian and a scientist and the author of a booklet, *The Christian and Science*. He discusses the charge that the creationist position is anti-science and anti-intellectual. He quotes Rudolph Bultmann who claims that the world-view of the Bible is mythical and that the Bible teaches a three-storied universe. Bultmann believes it is impossible to use electricity and radio and still believe in demons or spirits. Another quotation is from Stanley D. Beck of the University of Wisconsin, writing in the Autumn 1963 issue of *Dialog*. According to Beck, anyone who is reasonably well educated and informed cannot afford to disbelieve the system of evolution. He believes the principles of evolution are scientifically documented and anyone who accepts the creation position is unscientific and unscholarly. Then Zimmerman proceeds to show that the creation position is intelligent, scholarly, and scientific.

PAUL IN OPPOSITION TO SCIENCE?

At first glance it would appear from Paul's statements in I Corinthians 1:20 that the church does take an anti-intellectual and anti-scientific stand. He asks where is the wise (scientist), where is the scribe, where is the disputer of this world? He continues by saying that God has made foolish the wisdom of this world by the preaching of the cross. It would appear that Paul is placing science and scholarship on one side and the cross on the other; the two opposing each other. In the light of church history it is difficult to believe this is what Paul meant. We recall that Martin Luther established schools when there were none and our church missionaries have gone into many countries and established schools on all levels and hospitals where there were none.

THE CROSS IS CENTRAL

We found an answer to this problem in a study of many sermon outlines on this section of Scripture. They all stress the general thought that unless we have the cross, we have nothing. Again and again the refrain is repeated: I want to know nothing except the cross of Christ. This is valid reasoning, but does it rule out science and scholarship? Because Paul says that God has chosen the weak things of this world and its foolish things to confound the wise, must we be anti-intellectual? Not at all. It is the worldly wisdom which in its pride opposes the cross, that is condemned. This includes the theory of evolution which seeks to make a god out of time, chance, and environment and in pride rules out God and opposes the cross.

THE CROSS AND SCIENCE

The answer is that we must see the need for the cross in scholarship and in science, as well as in every other field of endeavor. It is important that we view the cross in our worship services, but it is also important that we see the cross when we study biology, geology, and other science disciplines. While we are studying a specimen under the microscope we should be concerned with having the knowledge of Jesus Christ and Him crucified. It is as important for a biologist to be aware of Christ while he is dissecting a frog as it is while he is dissecting a Scripture verse. The influence of Christ has always promoted science, and we should return His influence to education and to science.

REFERENCE:

The Christian and Science, by Paul Zimmerman, Bible-Science Assn., Caldwell, Idaho (1964).

13. SCIENCE MUST BUILD ON CHRIST
I Corinthians 3:11

In his book, *Man's Origin, Man's Destiny*, A. E. Wilder Smith compares the morals outlined by Christ with those proposed by evolutionists. He mentions particularly the morals as outlined in the Sermon on the Mount. "Blessed are the poor in spirit" runs counter to the evolutionistic theory of survival of the fittest which involves natural selection and merciless extinction of the weak. Christ's promise that the meek shall inherit the earth just doesn't fit into the evolutionist's plans. According to Jesus, the merciful shall be blessed, but survival of the fittest does not tend to make one merciful. The peacemakers shall be blessed and inherit the earth, but evolutionists support evolution and disorder.

JESUS CHRIST, THE FOUNDATION

In I Corinthians 3:11 Paul relates how the church at Corinth was built. He had planted, Apollos had watered, but it was God who gave the increase. The foundation was Christ. Paul distinguishes between a structure built with hay and stubble and one built with gold and silver, adding that only one built on the foundation of Christ is made of gold and silver. Outward appearance is immaterial—if it is not built on the foundation of Jesus Christ, it is but hay and stubble.

We are wise if we agree with Wilder Smith that all of science ought to be built on the foundation of Jesus Christ. Any science which is not built on Christ is developing a morality and a set of characteristics totally opposed to those presented in the Sermon on the Mount. In place of meekness there is pride and ruthlessness, for mercy there is extinction, and revolution replaces obedience.

BUILDING ON CHRIST

Christians are committed to building the sciences on Christ. In biology we recognize that God created life and preserves it. In an era where offspring are produced by means other than those of normal procreation we need Christ's principles of morality or we will create a chaos worse than that produced by hippies and rioters. Christ is needed in physics or the atom bombs and the more destructive bombs will be misused for utter destruction. Unless space research is based on Christ, we will miss the many blessings which it can offer.

REFERENCE:

Man's Origin, Man's Destiny, by A. E. Wilder Smith, Harold Shaw Publishers, Wheaton, Ill. (1968-1970).

14. THE GLORY OF GOD AS A TESTING STONE

I Corinthians 10:31

There is a conflict among Christians whether or not it is possible for a Christian to accept theistic evolution. We recently received an unsigned card stating that when we refuse to accept theistic evolution we box in God. The March, 1971, issue of *The American Scientific Affiliation* carried statements on this conflict, some voicing acceptance and some opposed. A scientist must be at least a nominal Christian to be affiliated with this group. One of the most vocal of these scientists who claims he is Christian and who strongly favors the theistic evolution view is Jan Lever of the Free University of Amsterdam. In 1970 he published a collection of nine television addresses titled, *Where Are We Headed?* Lever contends that by accepting theistic evolution he is according more glory to God, while those who do not accept this view are retarding science. It is his opinion that the Bible was written for people of non-scientific eras and therefore Genesis 1-11 cannot be taken literally. If we accept the position that the earth is a sphere rather than flat we have already discarded the literal interpretation of Scripture, he says.

GLORIFYING GOD

The testing stone as to whether or not theistic evolution is permissible within the Biblical framework depends on which position gives the greater glory to God. In the tenth chapter of I Corinthians Paul had to cope with the problem of eating meat which had been offered to idols. Was it permissible, or was it wrong? He stated that it was not wrong to eat such meat, but it was wrong to eat this meat in the presence of some who considered it wrong. He cautioned against offending the conscience of others. In verse thirty-one he establishes the general rule that whatever we do, we should do it to the glory of God. This applies to our daily tasks and includes science. Paul is saying that whatever glorifies God is right. We must honestly say that very little scientific research is carried on for the purpose of glorifying God.

ROMANS 1:25

At this point it seems to us the question is not whether or not we are boxing in God by refusing to accept theistic evolution, but whether by accepting it we are practicing idolatry. According to Romans 1:25 whoever worships the creature rather than the creator is guilty of idolatry which is paganism. Isn't this done in theistic evolution? Time is a creation of God and one of His greatest blessings, but it does not have creative powers as is suggested by theistic evolution. The environment is also a blessing and we note remarkable adaptations to environment in nature, but environment will not create even one amino acid, no matter how much time is allowed. Looking at theistic evolution from this viewpoint, it does not glorify God, but rather is in opposition to God.

FOUND WANTING

We could cite other arguments of Jan Lever such as fossils, contradiction of Genesis 1 and 2, and comparative anatomy, and disprove them all. When we recognize the essential paganism, the worship of the creature rather than the creator, the reliance on immense ages of time and development from lower to higher forms of life, and then apply the test of glorifying God, we find his position wanting. In fact, we are all found wanting. This is why we need a Savior who forgives our shortcomings, even the sin of idolatry.

REFERENCE:

Where Are We Headed?, by Jan Lever, Wm. B. Eerdmans, Grand Rapids, Mich. (1970).

15. THE RESURRECTION ARGUMENT AGAINST EVOLUTION

I Corinthians 15:38-41

In his book, *Life, Man, and Time,* Frank Marsh, biologist, reviews the history of thought since the days of St. Augustine on the meaning of the word "kind" in Genesis 1. Augustine followed Aristotle and took the position that there could be development. It is doubtful that he was a theistic evolutionist although Marsh believes he may have been. In his acceptance of this position he was followed by others, including Thomas Aquinas. Marsh believes that between the period 400-1600 A.D. the dominant worldview was a sort of theistic evolutionary one. Then came Francisco Suarez (1548-1617) who taught that God created fixed divisions in the plant and animal world with allowance for some variety within these main divisions. Then they swung too far in the other direction, and Linnaeus in his earlier years taught that all varieties were created fixed. Theologians at Cambridge followed his idea and taught this concept to Charles Darwin, a student there. When Darwin took his five-year trip around the world as a naturalist with a charting expedition, he discovered that there was a development of variety. He discarded the Bible and reacted by proposing that everything developed from a common source through natural selection. Today we look for a definition of the word *kind.* In his book Marsh refers to the phrase "after his kind" being used ten times in Genesis 1 as evidence that God did create the main divisions of plants and animals fixed as they now exist, with allowance for variety within the kinds.

PAUL'S POSITION

Support for Marsh's position which is accepted by most creation biologists is found in this chapter of I Corinthians where Paul cites arguments for the resurrection of the body. Some Corinthian Christians believed that only the spirit would rise, not the body. The purpose of this chapter is to show that our bodies will rise on the last day. In support of this position Paul shows that God made things to perpetuate themselves. Speaking of a seed, he shows that although when it is put into the ground, it dies so to speak, yet when it sprouts it produces a plant exactly like the one which produced the seed. So it is with our bodies. They will be changed into glorious incorruptible bodies, but they will be the very bodies we now have even though they may have been blown to bits at death. Paul indicates further that the flesh of man is distinct from that of animal life; it has always been different, and seemingly always will be. Paul even mentions bodies of things celestial. In verse forty he may be referring to angels, though some do not think of angels as having bodies. In verse forty-one he makes a clear reference to the sun, moon, and stars which retain their distinctive characteristics. Paul does not state specifically that the bodies of animals, fish, birds, or the sun, moon, and stars will be restored in the life to come. There is more indication of this in Romans 8:23. But he does stress that there always has been and always will be a difference; yet within the area of fixed relationships there is room for variety. In the life to come our corrupt bodies will become remarkably glorious.

MICRO-EVOLUTION

Here we find support for micro-evolution (the development of varieties within a kind) if we wish to use that term—but a strong argument against mega-evolution (the development of one major kind into another). It shows the impossibility of man evolving from the lower forms of life or of everything being the result of one amoeba or one euglena over a period of billions of years. The distinctions we note were present at the beginning and seemingly will continue to eternity.

Within these distinctive classes there is much room for change. If this were not the case, we could not hope to have a glorious body upon resurrection. Change does not include development from amoeba to man. This chapter presents a picture of what can and does happen, and what has never happened or will never happen. Christ's resurrection has proved that our bodies will one day be glorified.

REFERENCE:

Life, Man, and Time, by Frank Marsh, Outdoor Pictures, Anacortes, Wash. (1967).

16. EVOLUTION AND RESPECT FOR AUTHORITY

Ephesians 6:2, 3

Few people will disagree with the statement that we live in a permissive society, a society in which many do not respect authority. Many young people are vocal in demanding their rights. They have no respect for their elders; they engage in revolutionary tactics, often burning buildings. They refuse to work in a disciplined society. This lack of authority extends to the home, to labor relations, and even to politics. Is this good or bad? Some say it is good because it prevents repressing ourselves. Others disagree because they note the many evils which prevail as the result of such a society.

THE INFLUENCE OF EVOLUTION

John Moore, a science instructor and philosopher at Michigan State University at East Lansing, has written a tract titled, *Should Evolution Be Taught?* He shows that the general theory of evolution which embraces the billions of years and an amoeba-to-man development is more than a science. He demonstrates how this concept has been responsible for Marxism and Communism, Nietsche and Hitlerism, and the Frankfurter decisions of the U.S. Supreme Court. It is also responsible for the liberal theology espoused by Fosdick and others, and for the humanism which Huxley proposed. It is responsible for the progressive and permissive education concepts propounded by John Dewey. One of the main contributing factors to our permissive society with its attendant evils is the prevalence of the theory that man evolved from animal forms through a process of survival of the fittest. This concept upholds revolution as a virtue.

GOD'S POSITION

According to Paul, in this chapter, it is important that children respect their parents and authority. He even says their earthly happiness depends on having this respect. Paul does not accept the position that standards of right and wrong are the result of development and can be changed from time to time. It is his uncompromising opinion that God has determined a standard of right and wrong which is inflexible and permanent. We cannot go beyond this position and we do not believe that adherence to such a standard represses people. Conformity to God's principles is basic to earthly happiness.

THE CREATIONIST POSITION

Creationists uphold the position that we must submit to God's standard of the Ten Commandments and must show respect for authority. That so many reject this concept is proof that of ourselves we will not practice respect for authority; we must be motivated by our Savior.

REFERENCE:

Should Evolution Be Taught?, by John N. Moore, East Lansing, Mich. (1970).

17. THE WORD OF GOD AND THE MOON WALK

I Thessalonians 2:13

United States astronauts have more than once been on the moon, but most dramatic is that moment when Neil Armstrong stepped from the spacecraft to touch the surface of the moon, the first time man had accomplished this feat. Many have hailed this step as a great achievement for science and for socialism. In fact, one president of a state university cited this as proof that government, given the resources, can do anything.

In contrast are remarks by a Christian, NASA scientist Rodney W. Johnson, who is an authority on lunar bases. *Christianity Today* recently carried an interview with him in which he stated that the Bible had not yet caught up with the moon walk. What he meant was that Christians had not studied the Bible in connection with space science and were not providing scientists with proper moral direction. With this we agree. Christians tend to be traditional and so they have permitted the rapidly developing space science to proceed without direction from Scripture. Now the question is what to do about it.

THE SUPERIORITY OF THE WORD

In studying this chapter in Thessalonians we find that the word of God has the power of God and is superior to the word of men. The first step in establishing a space theology is to recognize the authority of Scripture. Because sin entered the perfect universe which God had created, we find danger and destruction in space along with a remarkable demonstration of God's power and wonder.

CONTAMINATED BY SIN

The next step is difficult. That involves recognizing that

everything in nature, limitless as it appears, is contaminated by human sin and contains no absolutes or unchangeable blessings. Most scientists are not willing to admit this. For them the secrets of space will explain everything, and they refuse to recognize its limitations and deficiencies.

The next step follows automatically. When we recognize that in spite of man's accomplishments in sending men to the moon, we need Christ's blessing for this and all other ventures, we will make Him central in our total life.

SPACE RESEARCH

The importance of acknowledging the superiority of Scripture is noted in the motivation of space research. The primary object of space research is to find life in space in order to prove the theory of an evolutionary development of life. So far no life in space has been found and many people are losing interest in the space program. If people were informed of the many blessings which have accrued to man on earth through research in space, they would eagerly support it. If this discipline becomes motivated by the superior Word of God as revealed in Scripture, we will see unbelievable advances in the future.

REFERENCE:

"The Bible and the Moon Walk," editorial, *Bible-Science Newsletter* (August-September 1969).

18. THE DIFFERENCE BETWEEN
SUBDUE AND FEAR

Genesis 9:2

All of a sudden nearly everyone is concerned with the environment. To evolutionists, environment is everything because they believe everything came about as a result of environment; on the other hand creationists ascribe to God the existence of everything. But creationists too are concerned with the environment, knowing that it is a gift of God, and this concern is expressed in the textbook, *Biology, A Search for Order in Complexity.* One unit of four chapters is devoted to a study of ecology and the preservation of environment. As stewards of God's gifts, Christians have a duty to preserve the environment. Whether or not this includes limiting human population is another matter.

SUBDUE

Before Adam and Eve sinned, they were instructed to subdue the earth (Genesis 1:28). This may sound strange at first, because why would it be necessary to subdue a sinless earth? Before Eve was created Adam had named all the animals, intuitively aware of the character of each. Is this what "subdue" meant before sin?

FEAR AND DREAD

This puzzle begins to clear when we read in Genesis 9:2 that the fear and the dread of man would be upon beasts, creeping things, birds, and fishes. There is a difference between fear and subdue; fear involves the influence of sin, while subdue might imply that nature sympathetically acceded to man's control by divine decree. Nowhere do we read that animals resented Adam's naming them, and the harmony which existed was such that the serpent talked to Eve in the Garden. After man's sin, a curse was placed on nature. Man has dominion over nature, but it is dominion of force, of fear and dread. The principle is established in Scripture that man is the crown of creation and that nature is tied in with him. We cannot say that nature is neutral or amoral, but since the contamination of sin, fear and dread of man has replaced the harmonious subduing of nature.

FORGIVENESS

Christ's forgiveness influences man's treatment of nature and his environment. This forgiveness leads Christians to live in harmony with nature and to treat it with concern.

REFERENCE:

Biology: A Search for Order in Complexity, by C.R.S., Zondervan Publishing House, Grand Rapids, Mich. (1970).

19. THE ORIGIN OF THE RACES

Genesis 9:19

The origin of the races is a topic of intense interest to many people. Intriguing questions are asked how the Caucasian, Negro, Indian, and Asian peoples came to be what they are today.

People who study this field are called anthropologists and most of them believe that man has reached his present state through a long, slow process of development and that environment plays a role in this development. Ordinarily they attempt to account for the various races in much the same way.

One anthropologist who takes a different view is Dr. Arthur Custance of Ottawa, Canada. He believes that there is scientific evidence for convergence, meaning that unrelated life forms facing the same needs in nature, will acquire some of the same structures. He uses an example found in Hardy's *The Living Stream.* The desert rat and the jerboa, though not related, both respond to the environmental pressure of loose sand by developing the ability to jump like a kangaroo. Dr. Custance applies this also to humans who develop certain structural forms to meet specific environmental needs. It is claimed that the Eskimo has a sort of keel on the top of his head; this extra muscle is needed to chew meat more vigorously. It is Custance's opinion that in early times the human form had a greater plasticity, responding to environmental needs, developing the various racial forms which have since become fixed.

The real point which Dr. Custance makes is that when convergence is allowed, we allow for purpose in nature, and this leads to a Purposer. This is what the natural mind tries to eliminate, for according to Romans 8:7 the natural mind is at enmity with God.

PEOPLE SCATTERED

Genesis 9:19 reports that the sons of Noah—Shem, Ham, and Japheth—and their descendants spread over the world. All mankind after the flood has descended from this family. Whether the earth was one or more continents is immaterial; people were able to migrate. There may have been one land mass, or the oceans may have been at lower levels, or there may have been more land bridges making the migration relatively simple.

POTENTIAL FOR VARIETY

Our knowledge of the gene structure of a cell nucleus indicates the possibility of the potential development of all the races from Adam's genes, or Noah's genes. From this potential God selects those genes needed to meet each specific environment as Custance's scheme of "convergence" suggests. The races were developed to meet certain environmental needs and are an example that God is a God of variety as well as of order. It should be stressed that the development of the races has been influenced by sin but is not necessarily an evil in itself. All racial differences are wiped out completely in Christ's atonement.

REFERENCE:

Doorway Papers (Convergence and the Origin of Man), by Arthur C. Custance, Ottawa, Canada, (No. 7-1970).

20. A MODERN TOWER OF BABEL?

Genesis 11:4

There were mixed reactions to the first U.S. moon walk. As reported in the *Bible-Science Newsletter,* Evangelist C. M. Ward of the *Revivaltime* radio program received several objections to his praise of the astronauts' achievement. One listener offered the opinion that this feat was purely secular and should not have been compared with anything religious. Another listener quoted Psalm 115:16 to support her contention that man should not venture into space. A minister fashioned a colored poster to portray man's limited knowledge, the moon walk notwithstanding.

SPACE RESEARCH AND THE TOWER OF BABEL

Sometimes our obsession with going farther and farther into space bears a similarity to the building of the Tower of Babel recorded in Genesis, chapter eleven. God had commanded the people to scatter and populate the earth, but they said "go to" and schemed to build a tower reaching to heaven in defiance of God and to prepare against His judgments. God also said "go to" and He divided their language and forced them to scatter. We do not know if this division of languages occurred during the days of Peleg, or prior to his time, or if there was a division of continents at that time and the people were scattered because of both language and land division.

We do know that the people building the Tower of Babel disobeyed the command of the Lord. There is no clear statement that space research and attempts to reach the moon, Mars or Venus are contrary to God's wishes. Adam and Eve were commanded to subdue the earth (Genesis 1:28), and it is implied that the universe is included. From Psalm 115:16 it is evident that man is not fashioned to dwell in space or on the moon; neither is he equipped by nature to live on the ocean bottom, yet his underwater exploration has led to many rich treasures. When man plunges into the depths of the sea or is rocketed into space, he must take along his earth environment. We cannot on the basis of Scripture condemn space research and exploration.

ABUSES

It is an entirely different matter when man's motivation for this exploration is to find proofs for the evolution of life and when he haughtily assumes all credit for successful ventures into space. Such motivation can be compared with the motivation of the people building the Tower of Babel. God disorganized them and disrupted their plans. So today man is not finding what he wanted to find—the moon is not habitable, there are no canals on Mars; Venus' temperature is too hot for life to survive; there is no evidence of water in space. God discredited the sinful motives of the people building the Tower of Babel; He is also discrediting the evolutionary theories of modern man.

Only when we follow the guidance of Christ and His word will our space research become a blessing.

REFERENCE:

"The Bible and the Moon Walk," by Walter Lang, *Bible-Science Newsletter* (August-September 1969).

21. GOD'S MERCY IN THE MIDST OF SCIENCE

Exodus 34:6, 7; Numbers 14:18; Psalm 103:8

In his series of filmstrips with accompanying booklets titled, *The Atom Speaks,* D. Lee Chestnut relates the Bible to nuclear science. He deals with the fear that unleashing the power of the atom bomb, the hydrogen bomb and the cobalt bomb will destroy the world's population. In contrast he points out how these newly discovered energies can be used to understand how God is holding together the atom (Col. 1:17) and the means by which He will dissolve the world at the end of time (II Pet. 3:11). He says that we need not despair or fear that man will destroy himself through atomic power, but should be encouraged to use the knowledge of nuclear physics for a better understanding of Scripture.

MOUNT SINAI

When God spoke like a trumpet from Mount Sinai, the people saw fire, felt the earth quake, and they were filled with fear. They asked Moses to speak with God, saying that if God spoke to them any longer, they would all die. People today fear the power of the atomic bomb; the Israelites feared the manifestations of God's power and glory. Moses returned from the Mount with the two tables of stone on which God had written the law. In his anger at the people for worshiping the golden calf, Moses broke the tables of the law. Once more he ascended the Mount carrying two tables of stone. As the Lord passed by before him, He uttered this beautiful expression, "The Lord, the Lord God, merciful and gracious, longsuffering, and abundant in goodness and truth, keeping mercy for thousands, forgiving iniquity and transgression and sin." Here is a description of God, the God of nature and the God of the covenant. God is merciful as a mother and gracious as a kind father. He is described as forgiving for thousands of generations, meaning thousands of thirty-years, a long time. God forgives all sin and all evil, nothing is excluded. It is no wonder that Moses repeats this promise when he pleads with God not to destroy the Israelites when they refused to enter Canaan (Num. 14:18). No wonder that the psalmist uses this expression in describing God's mercy (Ps. 103:8). This is a basic statement used throughout history.

SCIENCE

The fear of the atomic bomb is only one of many fears with which people today live. They fear the power of computers. They fear the ultimate results of research in genetics such as programmed conception and cloning or the "duplicate copy offspring." In the midst of the awesome forces which our generation is privileged to use, we have the same measure of that grace and mercy pronounced at Mount Sinai. This is our hope and assurance.

This assurance motivates us to use to the utmost the forces discovered and made available through scientific research for man's welfare and blessing, always aware of God's mercy.

REFERENCE:

The Atom Speaks, series of filmstrips and booklets by D. Lee Chestnut, distributed through Bible-Science Association. (1954).

22. GENETIC LOAD AND MARRIAGE
Leviticus 18:6-19

Chapter eighteen of Leviticus is the standard Scripture passage on forbidden marriages. Forbidden are marriages between parents and children, between sister-in-law and brother-in-law, between grandparents and grandchildren, between cousins. Most governments have followed these standards in making laws restraining certain marriages. One exception is given in Deuteronomy 25:5. This is where an Israelite was to provide an heir for a male relative who had died without leaving children. This was a special provision and did not invalidate the general rule that close relatives were forbidden to marry. Members of an immediate family were not to marry, nor those one step removed (cousins), or three steps removed (brother-in-law and sister-in-law).

GENETIC LOAD

Although there has been little questioning of these marriage prohibitions, it is only in recent times through studies in genetics that we understand the scientific reasons for these prohibitions. On pages 122-125 of the textbook, *Biology: A Search for Order in Complexity,* is a discussion of genetic load. It is estimated there are up to three hundred defective genes in the human species. Some of the serious defects caused are hemophilia, diabetes, albinism, phenylketonuria (resulting in feeble-mindedness), hereditary deafness, possession of extra fingers or toes, lack of certain fingers or toes, short fingers, congenital nightblindness, short limbs. Some of these are dominant, others are recessive. In some parents these traits are obvious, and in others they are hidden. This combination of genetic defects is called the genetic load.

Hitler attempted to build a super race through genetics, and he annihilated vast numbers of people of Jewish descent. Others would prevent persons with defects from marrying. Often defective children are born to parents with recessive defective genes, but if only one parent possesses a defective gene, the offspring will be a normal child. Thus it is wise from a scientific standpoint to prevent intermarriage between related persons.

THE WIVES OF CAIN AND ABEL

A standard question of the agnostic is, Whom did Cain and Abel, or at least Cain and Seth, marry? Obviously they married their sisters. Remember at that time there was no genetic load; this has resulted from a build-up of sin and of mutations. At that time in history there would have been no undesirable consequences of marriage between relatives.

HANDICAPPED CHILDREN

Some geneticists propose to eliminate or to avoid all handicapped offspring. According to I Corinthians:1, 2, God uses the weak things of this world to confound the wise. Handicapped people provide an opportunity to exercise love in Christ. If Christ could turn His death into a marvelous blessing, He can use a handicapped child for blessing also.

REFERENCE:

Biology: A Search for Order in Complexity, by C.R.S., Zondervan Publishing House, Grand Rapids, Mich. (1970).

23. HOMOSEXUALITY IS SIN

Leviticus 18:22

Dr. G. Archer Weniger of Foothill Boulevard Baptist Church in San Francisco distributes a mimeographed news-sheet titled *Blu-Print*. This pastor is a conservative who is informed on what is going on in our nation's liberal churches. He makes frequent references to Glide Memorial Methodist Church in San Francisco, where among other things, they conduct services for homosexuals and perform marriages between men. In an issue Dr. Weniger quoted Canon Hugh Montiefiore of the Church of England, then vicar at the church serving Cambridge University. He says: "Jesus might have been a homosexual. Jesus need not have been hindered from marriage by lack of money or possible mates. Women were His friends, but it is men He is said to have loved." This is an example of the lengths to which homosexuals will go to excuse their sin. Homosexuality is becoming increasingly common in our society, which has become pagan because of the prevalence of the religion of evolution. It is an illustration of Romans 1:25 where St. Paul says that when people worship the creature rather than the creator (in evolution it is time, chance, and environment), they will practice the gross sins which he lists in verses twenty-seven and twenty-eight, one of which is homosexuality.

THE DEATH PENALTY

In Leviticus 18:22 we are told explicitly that it is a sin for a man to live with a man, or a woman with woman. In verse twenty-three sexual intercourse with beasts is forbidden under penalty of death. Homosexuality is the sin which caused the destruction of Sodom and Gomorrah (Genesis 19) and this sin is still referred to as sodomy. This was also the sin which was at least partially responsible for the dividing of the kingdom after Solomon's death (I Kings 14:24). In Judges 19 is recorded the terrible civil war and destruction of the tribe of Benjamin. It began because men of the tribe of Benjamin wished to commit sin with a young man who was lodging in their village overnight while journeying to his home. Instead, they raped his concubine all night and by morning she was dead. In his anger the man cut his concubine's body into twelve portions and sent a portion to each of the tribes, thus initiating the civil war. In I Timothy 1:10 St. Paul states that the law is made also for the sin of defilement with mankind, meaning the government is to punish such an evildoer.

SOLUTION

How can we overcome this widespread attempt to justify and even glorify a sin which Scripture condemns as being as sinful as murder? The first step is to recognize why this is happening. Why do even so-called Christian churches glorify a sin which the Bible condemns? It is because we have permitted a pagan religion to become entrenched, a religion which maintains that the universe is billions of years old, and that man has evolved from lower forms of life. Many claim that Scripture is not a book of science and that it contains errors. We are now reaping the full results of such paganism. So-called church leaders are excusing even sins which the Old Testament political law punished with death. It is time that we cease our attempts to compromise with this pagan religion and begin to recognize its evil consequences on our society. Finally, the only real solution is to be found in our Savior, Jesus Christ, who will restore the perfection which once reigned in the universe.

REFERENCE:

Blu-Print, Foothills Boulevard Baptist Church, Oakland, Calif. (April 20, 1971).

24. ECOLOGY AND POLLUTION

Leviticus 25; Deuteronomy 15

In Francis A. Schaeffer's book, *Pollution and the Death of Man,* he quotes Lynn White, Jr., author of an article "Our Ecological Crisis." Mr. White lays the blame for this state of affairs upon Christianity. To White's pagan and evolutionistic thinking, man is a product of nature and is not to be considered superior to it. While it is true that Scripture elevates man above nature, it is not true that a Christian is contemptuous of nature. In Schaeffer's analysis, White embraces pantheism, which is making a god of nature. A Christian has high regard for nature, but he does not equate it with God; he gratefully considers it a blessing of God.

CHRISTIAN RESPONSIBILITY

In this book Dr. Schaeffer notes that a Christian has a relationship to both God and nature. Man is superior to nature, but he is also its steward. Environment has been given to us to use, not to abuse; its use is part of our stewardship.

Ecology is the theme of Dr. John Klotz, writing in a recent issue of *Lutheran Scholar.* He quotes Lynn White and also Ian McHarg in *Design with Nature* to the effect that the Christian account of creation is responsible for today's ecological crisis. In contrast is a quotation of Lewis W. Moncrief in *The Cultural Basis for Our Environmental Crisis* showing that the Christian approach is the best one in overcoming this crisis. The non-Christian world faces a more grave crisis; for example, the Mideast is mostly wasteland because its people did not observe God's command for preserving the land and the environment. Critics read the creation account and the command for man to subdue nature and read no further; and they misunderstand what they read.

SCRIPTURE VERSES

According to the Old Testament ceremonial law, every seventh year was to be a sabbath for the land. During the sixth year God would provide sufficient food to support the people for three years, sustaining them during the time the land lay idle. This does not sound like people fitting White's criticism. Further, the Israelites were to observe a Year of Jubilee, during which all debts were cancelled and property reverted to its original owners. White and his companions have no concept of this type of stewardship; it is utterly removed from their thinking. The Bible is way ahead of us with regard to problems of ecology.

BALANCE

Our ecological crisis, if there is one, has not been produced by Christians. It is the attitude of having an easy life which has led to our problems; and these problems will not be solved through pantheism or a pagan concept of man and nature. Christ alone through His Word presents the correct picture of man and his relationship to his environment.

REFERENCES:

Pollution and the Death of Man, by Francis A. Schaeffer, Hodder Paperbacks, London (1970).

Analyzing Causes and Solutions of Ecology Crises, by John W. Klotz, *Lutheran Scholar,* April 1971.

25. MORALITY AND SCIENCE

Leviticus 26; Deuteronomy 28

Francis A. Schaeffer is a philosopher who understands the basics of Christianity. In one of his books, *Escape from Reason,* he shows from history how people have attempted to evade God and morality. Many Christians have tried this evasion by dividing their lives; devoting one portion to the spiritual and separating the other from God. What this amounts to, according to Dr. Schaeffer, is that believers state in evangelical words what the unbeliever says in ordinary words. Christians, they call themselves, but they accept the world's viewpoint. This division of our lives, separating our moral life from our daily or vocational life, is called *dichotomy*. When this is done, Christianity disappears, and even real science disappears. Finally, all that is left is determinism and pessimism. Morality influences not only our spiritual life, but also the blessing of science. The title, *Escape from Reason,* was chosen to show that people are not as reasonable as they claim in their attempt to separate morality from science. They merely make an irrational leap which eventually ends in spiritual and scientific suicide.

BLESSINGS AND CURSINGS

Leviticus 26 and Deuteronomy 28 list blessings and cursings, reward for morality and obedience and punishment for immorality and disobedience. God is telling the Israelites that if they will obey His commandments, keep the Sabbath, and refrain from idol worship, He will send rain and a bountiful harvest; there will be peace from war even though they are outnumbered; they will have many children, much wealth and cattle; they will have blessing in the city and in the field. On the other hand, if they serve false gods, make their children to walk through fire, and

55

live in promiscuity as their heathen neighbors, He will curse them. He will withhold the harvest and their land will be laid waste; they will flee before their enemies; and if they persist in their evil, they will become captives in a strange land.

These chapters point up the connection between morality and material blessings. The idea that Scripture and things spiritual must be separated from our daily life, an idea which has become common within the Christian church since the days of Thomas Aquinas, is contrary to Biblical teaching. Biology is not a science which can be studied apart from Scriptural morals. The discipline of biology reveals effects of human sin, observed in the law of entropy, in disease, and death.

CHRISTIAN TASK

The task of Christians is to affirm that Christ must be total in a Christian's life (Col. 1:18). No segment is to be separated. Either Christ governs our total life, or that portion in which He is not preeminent opposes Him, and eventually we lose Him altogether.

REFERENCE:

Escape from Reason, by Francis A. Schaeffer, Inter-Varsity Fellowship, London (1968).

26. SCRIPTURE DIRECTING SCIENCE

Deuteronomy 8:3-4

In his book, *Science and Faith: Twin Mysteries,* Dr. Wm. Pollard has an excellent discussion of the atom. In addition to the neutrons, protons and electrons, he speaks of the photons, neutrinos, matter and antimatter. The description of the atom as a miniature universe of orbiting suns and planets has been expanded to include forces and magnetic wave patterns, even baryons and mesons. Finally, there is something in the atom which defies scientific explanation; this something demands thought, organization and direction, and we cannot understand it. At one time it was believed that science would eliminate God, but today's physicist admits that God is present in the organization of even one tiny atom.

GOD'S WORD

These discoveries by physicists illustrate what Moses meant in his instructions to the Israelites and what Jesus expressed in answer to the devil's temptation: man does not live by bread alone, but by every word which proceeds from the mouth of God. The Word of God is more important than matter, for it is God's thought communicated to the world.

It is interesting that Jesus overcame all temptations of the devil in the wilderness by quotations from the Book of Deuteronomy. It is small wonder that the so-called higher critics attempt to discredit this book, claiming that Moses is not the author. Still the authorship of Moses and divine inspiration for the Book of Deuteronomy stands.

DIRECTION OF GOD'S WORD

These are devilish claims that the Bible is not a book of science, that when Scripture is introduced into biology or

57

physics, these disciplines lose their objectivity. This passage from Deuteronomy 8:3-4 will serve us in our temptations, proving that Scripture and science do belong together and that Christ's forgiveness has a bearing not only on our spiritual life but includes even our study of the atom in physics.

REFERENCE:

Science and Faith: Twin Mysteries, by Wm. Pollard; Thomas Nelson, New York (1970).

27. SCRIPTURE AND SPACE

Deuteronomy 10:14; I Kings 8:27; Psalm 68:33;
Psalm 115:16; 148:4

Two essays by Christians in *Behind the Dim Unknown* discuss the vast reaches of space which astronomers are discovering and also their ignorance in this field. One author is Dr. Frederick H. Giles, astronomer-physicist at the University of South Carolina and the other is Dr. Harold Hartzler, mathematician and astronomer, Mankato State College in Minnesota. Much knowledge of our solar system has been ascertained in recent years; astronomers are amazed at the endless reaches of space, and they are conjecturing that perhaps space is curving back on itself. Even our most sophisticated computers cannot count the stars. These authors acknowledge that God is needed to control the order found in space.

SCRIPTURAL STATEMENTS

A study of Scripture indicates that its statements do not display the ignorance which many astronomers and space scientists would have us believe they do. In Deuteronomy 10:14 we are told that heaven and the heaven of heavens are the Lord's, and the earth also. In the original, the words are in plural form, indicating the limitless reaches of space. King Solomon quotes this verse in his dedication of the Temple in Jerusalem (I Kings 8:27). In Psalm 68 David says the Lord rides upon the heavens of heavens; the plural for heavens again signifying that Scripture was aware of the vast reaches of space. In Psalm 115:16 David states that the heavens are the Lord's but the earth has He given to man. Some people use this verse as an argument against space research. It is true that space is not made to be inhabited by man, and neither are the ocean depths; yet man is able to explore these areas and use their treasures.

HOW MANY HEAVENS?

Because the Bible speaks of heavens as being plural, we ask how many heavens are there? St. Paul speaks of being caught up to the third heaven (II Cor. 12:2). We generally think of the atmosphere as being the first heaven, space as the second heaven, and God's throne or dwelling place as the third heaven. The Bible's concept of plural heavens goes beyond what astronomers can observe or measure; it includes the spiritual heaven.

SIN AND GRACE

As we delve into space to learn its secrets, we acknowledge that the Bible has always known them, and we find that the influence of sin extends even into space. For the most profitable study of astronomy and space research, we need guidance from Scripture.

REFERENCE:

Behind the Dim Unknown, edited by John Clover Monsma, G. P. Putnam, N.Y. (1966).

28. MOSES' LAWS ON ECOLOGY
Deuteronomy 20:19; Leviticus 19:23-25

Writing in a recent issue of *Lutheran Scholar*, Melvin H. Zilz notes that while modern technology and industry have made life more comfortable, they have also created problems of pollution. He does not agree that Christianity is at fault as Lynn White contends in his article, *"The Historical Roots of Our Ecological Crisis."* According to author Zilz, White overlooks the Scriptural admonitions to be good stewards of the blessings which God has given us, which include caring for our environment. Tracing the ecological crisis back to Adam's fall into sin places the blame on man rather than on God. The ecological crisis will be solved best when the principles of Christian stewardship are applied.

TREES

To substantiate what Zilz claims, we have the regulations of Moses regarding destruction of trees in Deuteronomy 20:19 and Leviticus 19:23-25. Ordinarily, when a city was besieged, its trees were destroyed in great numbers. Moses forbade the cutting down of fruit trees to use for military embankments during a siege. Moses also commanded that the fruit should not be used until the fifth year of a tree's life, after it had been dedicated to the Lord. These are good laws preserving the ecology.

RESEARCH

Rather than encouraging research to solve the pollution and ecological crises, people like Lynn White attempt to use these crises to destroy the Christian religion. These same people often boast that modern technology has produced a world superior to anything which Christianity has ever produced. They do not use scientific research to its fullest extent to solve problems of ecology, for they would rather destroy Christianity. Through wise research and technology we can use the blessings of nature without over-using them.

Moses' directions were good; he did not forbid use of all trees, only the slow-growing fruit trees which were not replaced easily. Even in warfare this regulation was to be observed. Here is the real answer—a wise use of nature. Those who oppose all commercial use of land in primitive areas are over-reacting. With proper controls, the land can be used for both commercial and recreational purposes.

BALANCE

These problems should indicate the need for Christ to direct research in the field of ecology. He overcomes sin, and when sin is overcome, man has better judgment. Christ will enable us to make the most of our natural resources while at the same time avoiding pollution.

REFERENCE:

"Ecological Crisis—Twentieth Century Thorns," by Melvin H. Zilz in *Lutheran Scholar* (April 1971), St. Louis.

29. SCIENCE CANNOT BE SEPARATED FROM CHRIST

Ruth 1:16-17

D. C. Spanner, an instructor in botany at the University of London, contends that in light there seemingly is both wave motion and jerk motion at one and the same time. Therefore we can accept Scripture as being inerrant while at the same time accepting the theory of evolution. He calls this complementarianism. Others might label it *dichotomy*, which means that people separate their minds into two compartments, one for science and the other for the Bible. Spanner accepts the Bible as God's Word but at the same time holds that the six creation days are figurative, that Adam merely had a dream when Scripture states that God took a rib from him to fashion Eve, and that science has proved that man evolved from lower forms of life.

RUTH'S DEVOTION

The story of Ruth in the Bible is used in many ways. Ruth would not leave her husband's mother but vowed to travel with her, stay with her, accept her people, and be buried in the same burial ground. Above all, Ruth accepted Naomi's God as her God. Even though Ruth's statements were not made in connection with marriage, they are often used as a marriage text at weddings where husband and wife vow to remain with each other for life.

These words can also be applied to the relationship between creationism and science. We cannot separate God from science. Whether we conduct experiments with the microscope, solve mathematics problems with computers, probe into space with radio telescopes, study an atom in a cyclotron, or drill into mantle rock at the bottom of the ocean, we need God. In Colossians 1:18 we read that Christ should be preeminent in all things, and in Ruth we see a remarkable example of what this means. She permitted nothing to separate her from Jehovah and the promise of the coming Savior. Her devotion was rewarded as she became an ancestress of Jesus.

DEVOTION TO CHRIST IN SCIENCE

As Ruth permitted nothing to separate her from the true God, so we should not permit science to be separated from Christ. We cannot serve Christ with one compartment of our minds and serve evolution with the other, D. C. Spanner notwithstanding. God demands that we serve Him with our whole mind and heart, and we cannot say that we accept Scripture and at the same time hold the position that the universe evolved of itself. The two positions are contradictory.

Yet it is amazing how many Christians attempt this sort of dichotomy or complementarianism; it has become a major problem in the Christian church. Christ saved mankind at great sacrifice so that our service to Him might be all-inclusive. An example of such whole-hearted dedication we find in Ruth.

REFERENCES:

Creation, Evolution and the Christian Faith, by Richard Acworth, Evangelical Press, London (1969).

Creation and Evolution, by D. C. Spanner, Zondervan Publishing House, Grand Rapids, Mich. (1965).

30. CREATING A SUPER RACE

I Samuel 2:6-7; Luke 1:52-53

According to Dr. Bolton Davidheiser in *Science and the Bible,* scientists believe they will soon be able to develop a super race of humans through genetics. They hope to accomplish this through controlling heredity. According to their plans a woman will be able to select a frozen one-day-old embryo from a row of filed envelopes, making her selection on the basis of eye color and other features. Virgin birth will become common, they predict. Dr. Davidheiser claims that all such offspring will be females. He also notes that some theologians claim that children conceived in this manner would be sinless. Dr. Davidheiser also refers to cloning, the process through which it is proposed to reproduce exact copies of either parent. All this amounts to a considerable amount of boasting.

HANNAH'S PRAYER

In Hannah's prayer, preserved for us in the inspired Bible, we read that "The Lord maketh poor, and maketh rich: he bringeth low, and lifteth up." When Mary had been told by the angel that she, lowly Mary, would become the mother of the God-man Jesus Christ, she said, "He hath put down the mighty from their seats, and exalted them of low degree. He hath filled the hungry with good things; and the rich he hath sent empty away." The Lord has reserved to Himself the power to determine the kind of people born into this world, and He directs whether they will become rich or poor, lowly or mighty.

EXPERIMENTS

Have we forgotten Hitler's attempts to build a super race according to the evolutionary philosophy of Nietszche? Have we forgotten the immorality and the sins committed in exterminating many thousands of Jews in his attempts to build this race of super people? These same atrocities would take place if our pseudo-scientists were permitted to continue in their attempts to develop a super race.

THE SCIENCE OF GENETICS

All this does not mean that we should disavow the science of genetics; we merely assert a principle which we believe to be fundamental: science must be controlled when it goes beyond the restraints of the Ten Commandments. On the other hand, we should refrain from needless restraints lest we hamper true scientific breakthrough.

CHRIST

Sin can never be overcome through genetics, because it, as all science disciplines, is contaminated by sin. Only Christ can produce a super race, and these are the Christians redeemed by His blood.

REFERENCE:

Science and the Bible, by Bolton Davidheiser, Baker Book House, Grand Rapids, Mich. (1969).

31. ECOLOGY AND GENEROSITY

I Samuel 2:21; Luke 6:35

At a science symposium held at Dordt College in Sioux Center, Iowa, in October of 1970, both creationists and evolutionists presented essays, two of which concerned ecology. Dr. Frank Cassell, zoologist at the University of North Dakota and Dr. Delmar Westra, professor of biology at Dordt College, refuted claims of Lynn White who maintains that problems of ecology have been caused by the theology of Christianity. Both essayists stressed the importance of Christian concern in solving ecological problems, love for our fellow men and love in using the blessings of nature. Above all, we need to love God and to recognize that all good things we enjoy in nature are gifts from His loving hand and are to be used according to His will. This is stewardship. Because man has not practiced good stewardship, but has selfishly used nature for his own profit, we are faced with an ecological crisis.

HANNAH AND SAMUEL

Hannah is an example of a generous person. She was the second wife of Elkanah and had no children as Peninnah, the other wife, did. This was an affliction for Hannah, so she went to the Temple to pray for a child. After convincing Eli the priest that she was not drunk but was praying fervently, she received assurance from him that her prayer would be answered. In her prayer she vowed that she would give her firstborn to the Lord, and when Samuel was born she dedicated him to the Lord. At an early age he was taken to the Temple to be trained by Eli. Samuel became an esteemed judge of Israel and founded Israel's education system with its school of the prophets which made possible the later glory of King David and King Solomon. After giving her son to the Lord, Hannah saw him only once a year. The Lord then blessed her with three more sons and two daughters.

GOD'S PROMISE

Hannah is an example of the principle which Jesus stated in the Sermon on the Mount, that those who do good, expecting no reward, shall be called the children of the Highest. In Luke 6:38 Jesus promises that those who give will in turn receive abundantly, "pressed down, shaken together, and running over." It has been said that the fastest way to become a millionaire is to give away 90 percent of your income. Few do this, but it truly works.

GENEROSITY

This type of generosity is vital to efforts in controlling the ecology. The pagan philosophy of Lynn White does not face the stubborn fact that genuine love is needed for a proper management of the environment. Genuine love is possible only through Christ who loved His enemies with love so great it prompted Him to die for them that they might have eternal life.

REFERENCE:

The Christian in Science, Dordt College Symposium, Aaldert Menninga, editor (1970).

32. THE WEATHER OBEYS GOD'S LAWS

I Samuel 12:17-18

In Ecclesiastes 1:6 we read a description of how the wind travels south, then turns to travel north, following circuits. This is mentioned by James D. Worthington in a booklet titled *You're Speeding 18½ Miles per Second.* He also mentions meteorologist William Ferrell (1817-92), who formulated a law noting that the course of the wind follows the rotation of the earth. Because air is warmer at the equator and cooler at the poles, it ascends at the equator, flows to the poles where it is deflected, giving rise to the southwesterly anti-tradewinds in the northern hemisphere while in the southern hemisphere the flow is to the southeast. Matthew Fontaine Maury, father of oceanography, also discovered the air currents. These currents mix the air, carry vapor from sea to land areas, and tend to equalize temperatures on earth. There definitely are laws which control temperatures and wind patterns.

SAMUEL AND THE WEATHER

Many people today claim that laws governing temperatures and wind patterns are automatic, having developed over immense eons of time through chance and natural selection. Samuel called for thunder and rain on a given day to prove that the Lord was with him. When the thunder and rain came according to his request, the people realized that it is God who establishes and maintains the laws of weather, and He can direct them to suit His will.

IN GOD'S HANDS

There are numerous instances in Scripture where God controlled the weather at will. In Amos 4:7 we read that God withheld the rain when there were yet three months until harvest. God caused rain to fall on one city and not another; one piece of land received rain and another withered. It was God who smote their crops with blasting and mildew because Israel did not obey.

Fickle as weather may be, it obeys certain scientific laws. But behind the laws is God who controls them at will.

REFERENCE:

You're Speeding 18½ Miles per Second, by James Worthington, published by author at Atlanta, Georgia (1968, 1970).

33. PSALMS IN PLACE OF DRUGS
I Samuel 16:23

Dr. Lambert Dolphin, Jr., is a physicist working in research at Stanford University. At one time an evolutionist and a drug addict, he was led by the grace of God to accept Christ and is now presenting lectures in favor of creationism. In his book, *Astrology, Occultism, and the Drug Culture,* he describes the failure of the Haight-Ashbury experiment near the Berkeley campus of the University of California. In June of 1967 this was regarded as the heaven of the hippies. Poster galleries, coffee houses, and leather craft shops sprang up in place of usual businesses. People came for free love and drugs which were plentiful. When girls were forcibly raped and dope pushers were knifed, the grand experiment folded and is now completely dead.

SAUL AND DAVID

When King Saul disobeyed God and offered a sacrifice rather than wait for Samuel, God rejected him. An evil spirit came over Saul and no one knew how to overcome it. Then someone remembered that a shepherd boy, David, played the harp very well, and he was brought to play music for the king. Saul was soothed, and the evil spirit departed from him. Through this incident David received training in the king's court while he was still a boy, training that would be valuable later when he became king of Israel.

PSALMS

This account shows not only that good music is better therapy than free love and drugs, but it also teaches the value of the Psalms, the hymns of the Old Testament, many of which were composed by David. Not too many people have discovered that the Bible offers wholesome therapy for the emotional problems which led many young people to Haight-Ashbury. The Psalms are poetry that can help us curb our basic emotions which might lead to more serious problems and attempted drastic solutions. This is good psychiatry and certainly more effective than drugs.

CHRIST

The Psalms are also inspired, teaching the truths of law and order, obedience to the holy Ten Commandments, and salvation through the great Savior who was promised in the future. There is a psalm for nearly every emotion and occasion. If hippies would spend as much time in a study of the Psalms as they spend on free love and drugs, they could be doing great miracles for the Lord.

REFERENCE:

Astrology, Occultism, and the Drug Culture, by Lambert Dolphin, Good News Publishers, Westchester, Illinois.

34. TALKING WITH THE DEAD
I Samuel 28:20

A vivid account of spiritism and attempts to speak with the dead is given by Dr. Lambert Dolphin in *Astrology, Occultism, and the Drug Culture*. He tells of attempts made to talk with the dead at the Church of Satan, located in the Haight-Ashbury district not far from the University of California at Berkeley. Objects move mysteriously around the room during the seance. Unfortunately more and more people are turning to such superstitions, following the lead of Bishop Pike who had discarded belief in the Trinity, inerrancy of Scripture, and miracles.

SAMUEL AND SAUL

So we ask, What was it that Saul saw on his visit to the witch at Endor, just before going to his last battle with the Philistines? He thought he saw and heard Samuel who told him he would be with him the next day. Samuel was in heaven. This apparition was not Samuel, but it was the devil who is able to impersonate and to deceive. In Ecclesiastes 9:5 we read that the dead know nothing, and it is therefore impossible for the living to communicate with the dead. There is no doubt that the devil can and does impersonate the dead.

THE ARMOR OF GOD

Lambert Dolphin, himself a former drug addict, notes that it is important for Christians in their struggle against the devil to put on the whole armor of God as it is described by St. Paul at the close of Ephesians, chapter six. We need the breastplate of righteousness, the shield of faith, feet shod with the preparation of peace, and the sword of the spirit. Science is a great blessing, but these weapons needed to combat the devil are found only in

Scripture. Superstitions and attempts to communicate with the dead flourish in the atmosphere of paganism. We can overcome them by using the armor of God.

REFERENCE:

Astrology, Occultism, and the Drug Culture, by Lambert Dolphin, Jr., Good News Publishers, Westchester, Illinois (1970).

35. THE LORD'S PLACE IN HISTORY
II Samuel 7:9

Dr. Albert Hyma is a modern historian and author of the five-volume series, *History of World Civilization*. Hyma's approach is refreshing. He does not assume an evolution of man and that there is automatic improvement, nor does he promote a socialist philosophy. Author Hyma recognizes that God is the real force in history; that there have been cycles in history when He has blessed people and cycles when man has regressed due to his sins. In recording history it makes a difference whether you accept a creation oriented philosophy or an evolutionary philosophy.

THE GLORY OF DAVID

In this chapter we see David at the zenith of his power and glory. He truly was one of the great kings of the world. Nathan, the prophet, admonished David to remember that this success was a blessing of God. God had taken David while still a shepherd boy and given him a spirit of greatness and blessed him in all encounters with his enemies. David did not forget God while he was enjoying prosperity and success, but he remained humble and continued to give all glory to God.

HUMILIATION AND REPENTANCE

Many of David's psalms reveal a spirit of repentance. David had sinned grievously in taking another man's wife, but he repented sincerely. When one accepts the philosophy of evolution that development is achieved through imperfections, it is difficult to detect sin, and even more difficult to admit sin and repent of it. History does not record automatic development throughout the ages. On the contrary, history records that when people follow God's precepts, society prospers and civilization develops; when people disregard God's laws, society begins to decay.

Through modern science the Lord has richly blessed our generation but few people glorify God for modern successes as David did. We need more authors like Dr. Hyma. Theology can and does have absolutes and therefore theology should direct the sciences and philosophy as well.

SOLOMON AND CHRIST

Solomon not only had the proper balance between Scripture and science, but he had his own way of leading men to Christ, who was not born into the world until a thousand years later. He pictures Christ as the highest Wisdom who is able to open to man all the treasures of wisdom and knowledge.

REFERENCE:

The Christian Stake in Science, by R.E.D. Clark, Moody Press, Chicago (1968).

36. SPACE AND GOD

I Kings 8:27

Dr. Harold Hartzler is a mathematician and astronomer and executive secretary for an organization of Christian scientists. In the book, *Behind the Dim Unknown*, edited by J. C. Monsma, Hartzler writes about the vast reaches of space. The distance from the sun to the outermost planet is believed to be four billion miles and the distance to the nearest star has been estimated to be more than sixty-four thousand times as great. According to Dr. Hartzler, astronomers are doing a good deal of guessing, and the only part of space that we know very much about is our own solar system. Beyond this, astronomers are guessing and distances may not be as great as claimed. Regardless of exact distances, they are great enough to seem limitless to us. We sometimes ask how can God, who created these vast reaches of space and the numberless constellations, deign to deal with each individual on earth. The earth is but a tiny speck in a limitless sea of space, and each of us is but one of a great multitude.

FEAR OF GOD

Even with our advanced knowledge of space we still have a fear of it. There is concern over cosmic rays, radiation, and the many unknowns. The ancients, knowing far less of space, had a greater fear and often prayed directly to the constellations in the sky. At the dedication of the Temple at Jerusalem, the most costly building ever erected, Solomon used three words for the heavens, all of them in a plural form (I Kings 8:27). Solomon knew about the nature of space as did Moses before him (Deut. 10:14). God is above and beyond space, and therefore we should fear Him more than we fear space.

GOD AND MAN

Many people have the concept that the earth cannot be important because it seems to be such a tiny speck in the universe. And how can any of us really be important because we are such minute specks in a vast universe? This is the thought that Solomon expresses. This God who created all of space and everything in it is asked to dwell in the Temple which Solomon built. In the same spirit we ask God to be concerned with each of us and all our problems. And God does this. He can be Lord of everything in space and at the same time be intimately concerned about the problems of each of us.

In reality, the earth is not that insignificant. When we compare the vastness discovered within the atom or the life cell with the vastness of space, we note that the earth is in the center of these two worlds.

This great God condescended to become a babe in the manger, to live a sinless life of substitution, to die and rise again that we might have eternal life in perfection.

REFERENCE:

"Stars of Light and Problems of Great Darkness," by Harold Hartzler in *Behind the Dim Unknown*, edited by J. C. Monsma, G. P. Putnam and Sons, N.Y. (1966).

37. HOW MANY HEAVENS?

Genesis 1:8; (Matt. 6:9; II Cor. 12:2)

One of the strange statements in Scripture is the use of the plural form for "heavens." In Genesis 1:1 we read that God created the "heavens" and the earth. In Genesis 1:8 God called the firmament "heavens." It is remarkable how many times the term "heavens" is used in Scripture. Generally our translations use the term in its singular form. Even in the Lord's Prayer recorded in Matthew 6:9, "Our Father who art in heaven" is "heavens" in the original Greek. Why?

THIRD HEAVEN

In II Corinthians 12:2 we read that Paul was caught up to the third heaven in a vision and he was with the Lord and saw things not lawful to utter. Generally we think of the atmosphere, or the sky, as the first heaven; space is the second heaven; God's throne, or the spiritual realm, is the third heaven. Paul was in this spiritual realm.

The Bible is not opposed to scientific research in space. We have shot satellites into space and several men have walked on the moon. There is interest in reaching Mars and Venus and even exploring beyond our solar system.

THREE-STORIED UNIVERSE

Quite a number of Christians have suggested that the concept of the universe in Scripture is that of a three-storied universe. Rudolph Bultmann has suggested this view, and Dr. Paul Zimmerman notes that many follow his ideas. Terrence Fretheim also suggests this in his book, *Creation, Fall, and Flood.* He claims that the Israelites, and the Bible, picture the sky as a inverted bowl of solid material, and the Bible describes the firmament as something solid held up by pillars (Job 37:18; 26:11). Other references for pillar supports are found in Job 9:6; I Samuel 2:8; Isaiah 40:12 and Amos 9:6. But in Job 26:7, four verses before mentioning pillars, it says the earth hangs on nothing. We cannot interpret Scripture to teach that heaven is one story, earth is the center story, and hell the lower story. God is still stretching out the heavens as a curtain according to Psalm 104:2, Isaiah 40:22, and Job 9:8. Those theologians who claim the Bible teaches a three-storied universe have not studied it thoroughly enough.

GOD IS LIMITLESS

In nature, in science, and in Scripture we find a picture of a God without limits. All the remarkable discoveries being made in space have been there all along, and these only add to the power of the Bible. In Job 26:14 we read that the things in space are merely a whisper of God's power and then Job asks what must the thunder of His power be. The greatest measure of this limitless power is in Christ who is like the sun in its strength. (Ps. 19:4-6) and who has redeemed us.

REFERENCES:

The Christian and Science, by Paul Zimmerman, Newsletter (1964).

Creation, Fall, and Flood, by Terrence Fretheim, Augsburg Publishing House (1969).

38. REPRODUCING SEEDS

Genesis 1:11

An exciting area of scientific research today in the field of genetics is in the reproduction cell. The spectacular success of space exploration and the moon walks have been highly publicized, but few people are acquainted with the success of research within the life cell. When we understand this research, we appreciate more fully the statement of Genesis 1:11 that God made plants, shrubs, and trees with seeds in themselves. Fertilized seeds have powers similar to those of a fertilized life cell in humans.

COMPLEXITY OF A LIFE CELL

Instruments aiding the study of the life cell and revealing its complexity are the light microscope and the electron microscope. The light microscope magnifies to about one thousand while the electron microscope magnifies up to two million times. Within the life cell is a nucleus and a body, as there is a brain and body constituting the human being. Within the nucleus are the chromosomes each of which has entwined around it up to 2,000 genes. A human fertilized life cell may contain up to 100,000 genes, each of which has tremendous coding power. These determine in detail the later organisms. The cytoplasm also has coding power. In the cell body are the DNA and RNA acids, the latter serving as "messengers" and the enzymes which are compared with traffic cops. Then there are the ribosomes, one of which may contain up to three million molecules. The more we study the life cell, the more we realize its complexity, and the more we become aware of the wisdom needed in the creation of seeds and of reproductive cells referred to in Genesis 1:11.

REPRODUCTION POWERS OF A SEED

Even more remarkable than the complexity of a seed is the power to reproduce after its kind. There is very little in the environment which will change the coding established within the genes and the cytoplasm. Roses always produce roses even when surrounded by hawthorns. Yet a rose has a remarkable built-in variation potential enabling the production of many varieties. For more than a hundred years scientists have attempted to prove that environment is responsible for producing changes. From a thorough study of genes and chromosomes we see this is impossible. Environment can produce mutations through radiation and sometimes chemicals, but these changes are injurious to the life cell. Rather than developing new or improved kinds, they cause degeneration. Think of one race of mankind continuing for many generations and the many different types of plants and animals, each producing after its kind. When God created plants on the third day through His almighty word, He implanted this power of reproduction.

CHRIST AS A SEED

Jesus used Psalm 22, written a thousand years before He came, as a prayer on the cross. Verse thirty states that a seed shall serve Him and it shall be counted for a generation. Galatians 3:16 notes that the seed of Abraham is in the singular form, a reference to Christ. The power of a seed is great, but Christ has far greater powers. He gives us a new life.

REFERENCES:

The Creation of Life, by A. E. Wilder Smith, Harold Shaw Publishers, Wheaton, Ill. (1970).

Evolution and the Reformation of Biology, by Hebden Taylor, Presbyterian and Reformed Publishers, Nutley, N.J. (1967).

39. THE "KINDS" OF THE BIBLE
Genesis 1:11 (Lev. 11:22)

When Charles Darwin attended seminary he was told that the Bible teaches that all species of plants and animals were created fixed during creation week. This was the position of a scientist named Linnaeus, and the theologians claimed this is what the Bible taught. When Darwin made his five-year trip around the world in the "Beagle" he found many varieties of turtles and finches in the Galapagos Islands off the coast of South America. He was sure that these varieties had developed from one stock to fit the environment of the islands. He was positive that the Bible was wrong and he popularized the idea that not only was there development of variety, but that one major group could develop into another major group.

Did Darwin have a correct interpretation of the Bible? Frank Marsh, eminent biologist, shows in his book, *Life, Man, and Time,* that the Bible allows for the development of varieties. The first chapter of Genesis records that grasses, shrubs, trees, fishes, birds, and animals were all made after their "kind" and this word "kind" is used ten times. Sometimes it is difficult to determine even from the Bible what is meant by "kind." In Leviticus 11:2 a locust is distinguished from a bald locust by "kind" yet it is clear that these are no more than varieties. In science we see the development of varieties and we see the limits of this development. A development from one major group to another cannot be proved. Some have distinguished "kinds" by limiting "kind" to those creatures which can crossbreed, but this does not always fit. Clearly there are major "kinds" where development from one to the other cannot be accomplished.

CORN SEED

Dr. Walter Lammerts, geneticist and rose breeder, has shown that corn seed can be bred for higher yield, and this proves that variety is possible. But he shows that a limit is soon reached, following which the seed must be improved for qualities other than high yield.

MUTATIONS

Dr. Lammerts also explains mutations. Evolutionists depend on environment, natural selection, and time to produce not only new varieties, but also new kinds. Environment can cause a mutation but that is the sum total of the effect environment has on the hereditary portion of a cell. Mutations are produced generally by radiation or sometimes by a mustard chemical. In his rose breeding experiments Dr. Lammerts has induced many mutations from which to produce new varieties. Although this procedure will produce desirable varieties, it always produces a plant which is intrinsically weaker. Left to themselves these plants would have less survival value. Mutations are injuries to the life cell and cannot be a mechanism through which one major kind develops into another. We are still bound to believe that God created the original "kinds" fixed, as Genesis 1 states ten times.

As science catches up with the Bible, we see ever more clearly that the Bible is authoritative in all its statements.

REFERENCES:

Life, Man, and Time, by Frank Marsh, Outdoor Pictures, Anacortes, Wash. (1967).

"Discoveries Since 1859 Which Invalidate the Theory of Evolution," by Walter Lammerts, *C.R.S. Annual* (1965).

40. CREATION OF THE HEAVENLY BODIES
Genesis 1:14-16 (Isa. 30:26; Job 38:4, 7)

Christian scientists, particularly Christian astronomers, find their faith tested by the statement in Genesis 1:14-16 that the sun, moon, and stars were created on the fourth day, after creation of the earth. To most astronomers the earth seems to be a mere speck in the vast reaches of space, and they can't conceive of it being created before the extraordinary planets and galaxies of space. According to present day observations this does not seem logical. Light from distant stars, we are told, must travel many light years to reach earth; and one light year is said to be nearly six trillion miles. This information doesn't harmonize with the idea that these heavenly bodies were created after the earth was in existence.

POSSIBLE SOLUTIONS

Some have tried to solve this by saying that a cloud cover hid the galaxies and this cover was removed on the fourth day, causing them to appear. This position is favored by those who believe millions of years must be accounted for. Many who find a pre-world and its destruction in the first verses of Genesis believe that such a cloud cover was removed and that on the fourth day these heavenly bodies were assigned their tasks. They believe these bodies existed long before our earth was created.

THE WORD *MADE*

The words "let there be" in Genesis 1:14, 15 and the word "set" in Genesis 1:17 might allow for this assumption that the sun, moon, and stars existed previous to the fourth day and later became the means for regulating days, seasons, years. However, the word "made" in Genesis 1:16 will not permit this. This is a clear statement that these heavenly bodies were created after the earth and the heavens were created.

SCIENTIFIC CONSIDERATIONS

Dr. Walter Lammerts in an essay titled *"Discoveries Since 1859 Which Invalidate the Theory of Evolution"* indicates that the creation of "light" in Genesis 1-3 might be the creation of energy, including that of the stars. That is, in the beginning God created the light and energy and on the fourth day He converted some of this light and energy into constellations in space.

CREATION AND PRESERVATION

Creationists maintain that the creation of the world, including that of the heavenly bodies was accomplished through a different process from that which is observed today. According to Psalm 33:9, God spoke, and it was done. God does not work in this manner today. Following these different laws God could easily create the heavenly bodies after He had made the earth. Another example of different laws from those found in science today is observed in the miraculous rebirth which we have in Christ (John 3:9).

REFERENCES:

Discoveries Since 1859 Which Invalidate the Theory of Evolution, by Walter Lammerts, *C.R.S. Annual* (1964). Available in tract form.

41. DEFINITION OF "CREATE"

Genesis 1:21 (Isa. 43:1, 7)

There are those who belabor the distinction between words used for the origin of the universe and the origin of its parts. In Genesis 1:1, 21, 27 the word "created" is used. The word "make" is used in Genesis 1:7, 16, 25, 26; 2:2, 3, 4. The words "let there be" are used in chapter 1:3, 9, 14, 15. The expression "bring forth" is used in verses 11, 12, 20, 24 of chapter one. In Genesis 1:17 the word "set" is used while the word "formed" is used in Gen. 2:7, 19 and in Isaiah 43:1, 7. Everything in the Bible, including distinctions between words, has meaning and importance.

THE MEANING OF *CREATE*

Does the word *create* always mean to make something out of nothing? That is a good definition of *create* as it is used in Genesis 1:1. However, we are not sure the definition is appropriate for Genesis 1:21 where the reference is made to the creation of whales. There it is not distinctly stated that whales, the first animal form of life in the creation process, were made out of water, but it is definitely stated that God by His word caused fish to come forth from the water. When we come to the threefold use of the word *create* in Genesis 1:27, it is clearly stated that Adam was formed from the dust of the ground, that is, from preexisting material. We cannot say that *create* always means to make something out of nothing.

SYNONYMOUS USE OF *CREATE AND MAKE*

Those who believe in a pre-world, possibly millions or billions of years ago, and that this world was destroyed when the angels sinned, stress the difference between *create* and *make*. They contend that *create* means to make something from nothing and that *make* means to produce something from preexisting materials. According to this concept, when God "made" the sun, moon, and stars which He "set" in place (Gen. 1:17), these heavenly bodies were already in existence and God either removed a cloud cover to reveal them or He now made them to be light holders, setting them in place to be for days, seasons, and years, and signs. In Genesis 2:2 we are told that God rested from "all" His work which He had "made." Isaiah (43:1, 17) uses the three words synonymously, each referring to the same act; create, make, and form. We believe that, although there are distinctions between the words *create* and *make*, they can be used for the same act of God to make something from nothing. God may have made the heavenly bodies from preexisting material, but He did make them on the fourth creation day.

MAKE FOR THE FIRST TIME

Robert Reymond, the author of the monograph, *A Christian View of Modern Science*, suggests that if we wish to make a proper distinction between *create, make,* and other words, we should stress that *create* means to make something for the first time. This may be the solution. Primarily we should emphasize that everything came from God and has purpose. This original world was created in perfection. That perfection was lost through sin. Thanks be to Christ who recreates us in His righteousness!

REFERENCES:

A Christian View of Modern Science, by Robert Reymond, Presbyterian and Reformed Publishing, Nutley, N.J. (1964).

The Bible and Modern Science, by Robert Reymond, Broadcast No. 72, Bob Jones Radio, Greenville, S.C. (1970).

42. CAN SCIENCE CREATE LIFE?

Genesis 1:24 (Ps. 30:9; 63:3; 104:30;
Isa. 43:15; Acts 17:25)

In 1967 Drs. Kornberg and Goulian performed an experiment in which they took apart a virus, rejoined the parts outside the life cell, and the virus duplicated itself. Many people hailed this as unlocking the secret of life. A virus is not life, however, for it needs a host cell in order to live. This was a controlled experiment using living material and regulating the environment. These scientists did not produce life from non-living material.

In mid-1970 Dr. Khorana and his associates performed an experiment in which they synthesized a gene. A gene is the chemical which produces the coding in the chromosomes and in the nucleus, determining each detail of the later organism. This was a significant achievement, but it was not creation of life.

Perhaps in the future life will be created, but at this point in research it seems highly unlikely. The more that is learned, the more it is discovered how minute this knowledge is.

WHAT IS LIFE?

The life cell is a highly complex structure. It consists of a body and the nucleus, with the nucleus containing chromosomes and genes and these are a world in themselves. There are also many chemicals and the protein factors which are made up of as many as 3 million molecules. Enzymes number possibly 300,000. Then there are the DNA and RNA. The really significant thing about life is the coding system of the genes, for there can be no life without them. We do not understand what organizes their coding; surely it could not have arisen by chance. All man's intelligence and equipment have not been able to duplicate this coding of the genes.

THE BIBLICAL VIEWPOINT

What we cannot even understand, God created with His word. His word was all that was needed to produce these highly organized systems. In Psalm 36:9 we read that God is the fountain of life and in Psalm 63:3 that God's loving kindness is better than life. According to Psalm 104:30, God's spirit creates life and Isaiah (42:5) says that God gives breath to people and spirit to them that walk on the earth. In Acts 17:25 we are told that God gives life and breath to all things. Perhaps the Bible does not rule out that man will create life, but it states very clearly that God creates and sustains life.

The Bible goes even further. It says that the real life is spiritual life. John 10:10 tells us that Christ came so that we could have not only life but also the abundant life.

REFERENCES:

"Kornberg, Viruses and the Creation of Life," by Duane Gish, Bible-Science Newsletter (Feb. 15, 1968).

Evolution and the Reformation of Biology, by Hebden Taylor, Presbyterian and Reformed Publishers, Nutley, N.J. (1967).

The Creation of Life, by A. E. Wilder Smith, Harold Shaw Publishers, Wheaton, Ill. (1970). News clipping on creation of artificial yeast gene by Khorana, *Newsletter* (July 15, 1970).

43. IS VARIETY A PROOF OF EVOLUTION?

Genesis 1:25

Recently a creation-evolution debate was held at a midwestern high school. A Christian high school teacher and a pastor upheld creation while evolution was defended by a high school science teacher and a university professor. The evolutionists claimed that variety can be demonstrated and this was proof of evolution. There are varieties of horses, many varieties of roses, and much development in the corn seed. No one denies this. However, their next point was extrapolation. Because limited variation is observed, it cannot be proved that unlimited variation by development from one major kind to another can or did take place. Evolutionists need a great deal of faith to believe in the development of major kinds when the sum total of proof they have is a limited variety within a kind.

THE SCRIPTURAL POSITION

Darwin was taught that the Bible teaches the fixity of species, allowing for no variation. This was the scientific position proposed by Linnaeus and theologians interpreted the Bible to agree with it. Darwin did not realize that he had been taught an incorrect interpretation of the Bible, and so he rejected the Bible.

MEGA-EVOLUTION AND MICRO-EVOLUTION

To distinguish between legitimate development of variety and the unprovable development of one major kind to another, we sometimes speak of micro-evolution as referring to the development of varieties. Mega-evolution refers to the development of one major kind to another. Some creation scientists don't like to use the word *evolution* at all, but we use it here to distinguish between variation within a kind and development from kind to kind. Scripture allows for variation, but Christians know there is no proof for development (evolution) of one major kind to another.

The order and complexity and variety in nature reveal the wisdom and power of our great God who should be praised and glorified for His creation and for His redemption.

REFERENCES:

"*Discoveries Since 1859 Which Invalidate the Theory of Evolution*," by Walter Lammerts, *C.R.S. Annual* (1965).

Life, Man, and Time, by Frank Marsh, Outdoor Pictures, Anacortes, Wash. (1967).

44. THE BLESSINGS OF CHILDREN
Genesis 1:28 (Ps. 127:3; Gen. 9:1)

A recent issue of *Bible-Science Newsletter* discussed the topic of overpopulation. God's commands to Adam (Gen. 1:28) and Noah (Gen. 9:1) to beget children came under scrutiny. One pastor maintained that these were not commands but promises—statements coupled with a blessing. Therefore, it would not be an act of disobedience to limit the size of one's family.

In these passages there is both a command and a promise. Adam and Eve, and later Noah and his wife, were told to multiply and fill the earth. The King James version uses the word *replenish* which is not a good translation of the Hebrew which really means "to fill the earth." This is not an implication that a world existed prior to Adam and Eve.

In Psalm 127:3 children are called "an heritage of the Lord: and the fruit of the womb is his reward." Abraham and Sarah, Hannah, Zacharias and Elizabeth felt cursed because at an old age they had no children.

THE LORD'S BLESSINGS

People who speak fearfully of overpopulation do not recognize the Lord's blessings. Too often owning a new home or a new car is thought to be more important than having a child. A child is another soul to be redeemed by Christ and to live forever in heaven. The Bible says that one soul is more important than all the treasures of the world. It has been proved scientifically that animals and insects and fish have built-in population controls. Shall we doubt that God can and does control human population?

When we recognize the blessings of children and the sanctity of human life, we will appreciate the miracle of a life and soul brought into the world.

REFERENCES:

"Population Control, Evidence of a Perfect Creation," by E. Norbert Smith, *C.R.S. Quarterly* (Sept. 1970).

45. WERE ADAM AND EVE VEGETARIANS?

Genesis 1:29 (Gen. 9:3)

In *The Bible, Natural Science, and Evolution,* Russell Maatman makes the suggestion that death existed prior to the fall of Adam and Eve. If this is true, Adam and Eve may have been meat-eaters and animals could have destroyed one another.

In Genesis 3:3 Adam and Eve are told that they will die if they eat of the forbidden fruit. This implies there was no death at that time. Sin caused death and drastic changes in nature. The serpent was changed, and thorns and thistles infested the ground. Death was the punishment for sin. According to Romans 5:12 sin entered the world through one man, and death by sin; in the seventeenth verse we are told that life also came into the world by one man, namely Jesus Christ. These passages support the view that death is the result of sin and that there was no death before sin.

VEGETARIAN DIET VS. MEAT DIET

Following the flood, God commanded Noah to eat meat. Since death had influenced man, nature, and the animal kingdom, there was no particular advantage to refrain from eating meat. Prior to sin and death, only plant food was eaten. Since God permits the eating of meat, man can make a choice if he wishes. During World War I the Germans found that animals in their zoos thrived on a vegetable diet when no meat was available for them.

Some people claim that no meat was eaten until after the flood. It is recorded in Scripture that Abel offered a sacrifice of sheep, implying that sheep were slain and that their meat was eaten. There is no definite statement regarding meat in the diet. God permits the eating of meat in our sinful world and the animal kingdom's population is kept under control partially by death, but death is a curse and not a means of progress. Real progress is achieved only through Christ who has removed the curse of death and is the source of a new life.

REFERENCES:

Medical Health and the Bible, by George Howe, sound tape of essay at Creation Seminar, Lucerne, Calif. (July, 1970).

Life, Man, and Time, by Frank Marsh, Outdoor Pictures, Anacortes, Wash. (1967).

46. WORK IN THE GARDEN OF EDEN
Genesis 2:15

Christians maintain that God created a perfect world, that this world was perverted by sin, that it has been reconciled by Christ, and that there will be a new heaven and new earth where righteousness shall dwell. Then we ask how much different will this new heaven and new earth be? Will it be like the Garden of Eden? Many who labor hard and find it distasteful ask whether there will be work to do in heaven. Some hope it will be a place of complete rest and no work.

We know that Adam and Eve worked even before they sinned. In Genesis 2:15 Adam is commanded to dress and keep the garden. This was work. It was not drudgery; but it was work.

WORK IN REST

Adam and Eve worked, but they found rest in it. God used a tremendous amount of energy in His creation. He is still working in His preservation of the universe, but compared with the creation, it is resting. God rejoices in His work and He never tires. So it was with Adam and Eve. They worked in the garden, but it was never discouraging or unpleasant.

SIN AND WORK

Today things are different. Work is unpleasant; there is friction and even quarreling. Everything runs down, nothing ever stays put. There is death and destruction. It is not the running of the wheels that wears them out; it is the friction. After their sin, Adam and Eve were told that they must eat their bread in the sweat of their brow.

CHRIST AND WORK

Through Christ we can work in this life as though we were already in heaven. We can learn to turn troubles into blessings, and we can learn to live above our circumstances. When we become weary, we can be renewed through Christ's forgiveness, and we have the Bible to help us. We already possess the blessings of heaven in part and know that we will enjoy them in full measure in the life to come.

RESEARCH

Sometimes people will question the wisdom of our nation's space research. They believe it is an interference in God's affairs. God has commanded man to subdue the earth and to have dominion over the universe, and this includes space. Christians should be eager for research which glorifies God and upholds the accuracy of His Word.

REFERENCE:

Science and Christian Faith, by Wm. H. Davis, Biblical Research Press, Abilene, Texas (1968).

47. WHY WERE ADAM AND EVE TESTED?

Genesis 2:16, 17

Some things we will never understand, and one of these is why it was necessary for Adam and Eve to be tempted. We can understand that for man to be a responsible individual he must overcome temptation. We know, too, that the test was really quite easy. It is possible that also the angels were tested but we are not told what the test was. But why didn't God just make man and angels confirmed in their perfection?

God is not the author of evil and He gave His own Son to overcome that evil. But He has not revealed the reason for the necessity of the temptation, and it is something we will not understand in this life.

CONTINUAL TESTING

Since the advent of sin, this world is a place of continual testing. This is true also in the scientific disciplines where progress does not automatically result from making a certain number of observations, and deducing hypotheses, theories and laws. Progress is achieved only at the cost of much testing with minds and materials, where at least 95 percent of the ideas are discarded. This testing is basic to scientific progress.

Abraham's faith was tested when he was commanded to sacrifice Isaac. David was put to the test when Saul repeatedly tried to kill him. Paul had his "thorn in the flesh." Jesus underwent the supreme test in the Garden of Gethsemane and on the cross. Wherever we go, we are tested. Senior citizens like to think that after retirement they should be free from this testing but they find to their dismay that it goes on until death.

THE VALUE OF TESTING

There is definite blessing in this testing for it serves as a refining process (II Cor. 3, 4). The pages of the Bible, the history of the world, and of science are filled with examples of progress achieved through testing. Remember the testing which the astronauts endured in the 1970 moon shot when an explosion rocked their spacecraft, and they wondered whether they would make it back to earth! In heaven we believe there will be no testing, for we will be in the time of fulfillment.

TESTING IN CHRIST

To obtain its greatest blessing, testing in science or in our Christian life, should be centered in Christ. When He cried "My God, my God, why hast thou forsaken me?" He was suffering hell itself (Ps. 22:1 and Matt. 27:46). When He said, "It is finished" He had won the victory, and He rose from the dead to prove it. What really counts in scientific research is the determination to overcome the difficulties and to pass the test. Nothing will assure us of victory as much as the knowledge that Christ has overcome for us.

REFERENCE:

"*The Scientific Method,*" by John Klotz, in *Evidences for Creation,* Bible-Science Association (1968).

48. RELATION OF ENVIRONMENT TO CREATION
Genesis 2:19

From the mega-evolutionary standpoint, environment is all important. It was the environment in the primordial sea—gases such as methane, ammonia, hydrogen, and water vapor—which by chance combinations formed the first amino acids. By accident and by natural selection, also based on the environment, these acids combined to form a simple life cell, which as the result of environmental influences developed into ever higher life forms.

ENVIRONMENT AND CREATION

Environment played an important part in creation (Gen. 2:19). Animals and birds were formed from the dust of the ground, and the water brought forth living creatures in the sea (Gen. 1:20). Even man was formed of the dust of the ground (Gen. 2:7).

FROM INORGANIC TO LIFE

The modern scientist reaches an impasse in his experiments to create living material from inorganic material. The deeper the life cell is probed, the more we realize its complexity. Biologists speak of 3 million molecules in one ribosome, of 300 enzymes in one life cell, and of 100,000 or more genes within the nucleus. This is only the beginning. When scientists try to determine what it is that organizes all this complexity to form life with the ability to reproduce, they are stymied. Christian creationists know that life is far more than the sum of these parts, that life is something which cannot be put into the test tube.

What man cannot do or cannot even understand, God brought forth by merely speaking a word. All our microscopes, telescopes, electron microscopes, and computers have not explained what life really is.

ENVIRONMENT AND GOD

We should realize that environment is definitely a factor in the creation and composition of life forms, but environment cannot of itself produce life. If modern science, aided with a vast array of complicated instruments, cannot even understand life, much less create it, surely we cannot believe that chance environmental forces could produce life. It is God who adds the unknown ingredient, He organizes the individual parts, He produces life, and He provides the power of reproduction. In Christ we have something even more miraculous than the original creation of life. He recreates life which has been contaminated by sin and changes the environment into blessing.

REFERENCE:

The Creation of Life, by A. E. Wilder Smith, Harold Shaw Publishers, Wheaton, Ill. (1970).

49. THE SANCTITY OF MARRIAGE

Genesis 2:24

In our day there is controversy over "sex education" and the accompanying sensitivity training in the schools. Some claim that since parents are not providing this instruction for their children, it is up to the school to offer courses in sex education. On the other hand, many individuals claim that sensitivity training is an attempt to break down the sanctity of marriage and that we dare not develop a set of new morals to replace the Ten Commandments. Many of those who favor the teaching of sex education and sensitivity training imply that old rules about marriage are outmoded and permissiveness is called for.

THE RESULT OF EVOLUTION

People who understand that evolution is really a pagan religion which worships the creature rather than the creator are not surprised at these developments. Evolution refuses to acknowledge the true God and replaces Him with chance, time, and environment. As a result aberrations which are prevalent in the teaching of sex education and sensitivity training are becoming commonplace. Romans 1:28-32 is a good description of such conditions. According to evolution there must be continuous improvement, and these innovations are supposed to be improvement.

It is admitted that parents have neglected their duties in this respect, and that sex education can be taught properly. Group psychology can also be useful, but there is no excuse for using these methods of education to destroy obedience to the Ten Commandments.

THE SANCTITY OF MARRIAGE

During the Middle Ages the idea was prevalent that it was more holy to remain unmarried and to devote one's self entirely to church work than to be married. In our day there are those who claim that as a result of our so-called progress, the Ten Commandments, including the injunction, "Thou shalt not commit adultery," are outmoded. In either of these instances, the sanctity of marriage is destroyed.

Genesis 2:34 commands that a man shall leave his father and mother and shall cleave unto his wife, and they shall be one flesh. Because it is a part of creation, sanctity is attributed to marriage. Jesus refers to this in Matthew 19:3-9 to condemn the liberal divorce laws of the Pharisees. In the fifth chapter of Ephesians Jesus calls Himself a bridegroom and the church His bride. This illustration could not be used if there were anything sinful about the marriage relationship.

This again points up that the evolutionary position has moral implications as well as scientific ones.

REFERENCE:

Beware Sensitivity Training!, by Phoebe Courtney, New Orleans, La. (1969).

50. A PERSONAL EDUCATION
Deuteronomy 6:7-9

R. J. Rushdoony, the author of *The Messianic Character of American Education,* describes the work of John Dewey and his energetic and dedicated follower, George S. Counts, neither of whom felt bound by laws when developing a philosophy of education. Dewey was opposed to an "inner life" concept and believed that religious training and culture were futile, and there was even something rotten about such notions. To these men the ultimate in education was an impersonal something, for they believed that when the universe is ultimately and essentially impersonal, man and his society are at their highest state of development. This is the reason for their stressing socialism, an approach used by the communists. One of their goals was to abolish history records which stress individual achievement, and they sought to submerge the individual into the group. Despite the fact that Communist Russia and Communist China are our national enemies, our national school system is promoting a Marxist approach in education.

THE ATTITUDE OF MOSES

Deuteronomy 6:7-9 presents some of the greatest education maxims ever expounded. Speaking under inspiration and after a lifetime of study and experience, Moses stressed that the most important thing in life is to serve the Lord with all our heart, soul, and mind. To Moses, the most important element of our life is to have a personal relationship to God and to develop our inner life accordingly; this is the opposite of the philosophy of Dewey and Counts. Moses stresses the inner man by commanding the Israelites to keep God's law in their hearts, and he urges a continuous teaching in the home. He urges them not to turn from the unchangeable commandments either to the right or to the left. This is in sharp contrast to the philosophy which has shaped our nation's system of education.

CREATION CONCEPTS

Some people believe they can accept evolution and still maintain their Christianity. When we note the contrast between the philosophy of Dewey and of Moses, we realize that it is necessary for a Christian to renounce evolution, theistic evolution included, and all theories of immense ages whether embraced in evolutionary eons or pre-world gaps. Acceptance of such theories produces the impersonal and socialistic type of education which leads to renouncing God's holy Ten Commandments.

The basis of the gospel is that God's law is inflexible and man's inner life, the attitude of his heart, is of primary importance. Man's created perfection can be restored only in the substitutionary atonement of our Savior.

REFERENCE:

The Messianic Character of American Education, by R. J. Rushdoony, Craig Press, Nutley, N.J. (1963).

51. CHRIST, A SCIENTIST LIKE UNTO MOSES

Deuteronomy 18:15

Among several interesting studies on Christ's virgin birth is one by Dr. Arthur Custance of Ottawa, Canada. He shows that, although this was a miracle, it was needed for Christ to become human. As Christ was born a perfect human, so Adam was created a perfect man and did not evolve from the ape family. How could Christ be the second Adam if the first Adam evolved from the apes? Dr. Custance also notes that Eve, being formed from Adam's rib, carried the same genes as Adam. Thus, all mankind bears Adam's genes, also Jesus Christ in His human nature. This fact permitted Him to substitute for the whole human race in His atonement.

In Study No. 37 of *Science and the Bible,* Dr. Bolton Davidheiser mentions that it is possible for a male bee to produce offspring without the benefit of a female bee and that female turkeys and chickens are able to produce offspring without male participation. This is called *parthenogenesis.* Among bird species such offspring is always male and in mammals the offspring is always female. This, however, does not explain the virgin birth of Christ, for although He was born of a human mother, He was altogether without sin.

Whatever may be our scientific opinions regarding the birth of Christ, it must be admitted that Christ took on human flesh, thereby indicating that He came to redeem the flesh as well as the spirit. Christ's atonement includes the discipline of science as well as the scientist and He is, in fact, the world's greatest scientist. In the first chapter of John's Gospel we read that Christ created all things, and in Colossians 1:17 that by Him all things consist. Hebrews 1:3 says that He upholds all things by the word of His power, and according to Colossians 1:20, He reconciles all things.

MOSES AS A SCIENTIST

Deuteronomy 18:15 is a Messianic prophecy; God promises to raise up a prophet like unto Moses to whom all people should listen. At Christ's transfiguration Moses appeared with Him, and God spoke from a cloud, repeating the words that everyone was to listen to Jesus.

In a book of sermons written in 1891, Dr. C. F. W. Walther, an American Christian leader, devotes one sermon to the similarities and dissimilarities between Moses and Jesus. Moses was a prophet; so was Jesus. Moses spoke directly with God; so did Jesus. Moses was a mediator, a deliverer, and an advocate; Jesus likewise was all of these.

There were, however, notable differences. Moses gave the law to the world; Jesus gave it the gospel. Thunder and lightning accompanied Moses' law, and his law was destroyed. Jesus was comforting and peaceable, and He saves. Moses demanded holiness; Jesus gives it.

One set of comparisons Dr. Walther did not mention. Moses was a scientist describing creation, the flood, the origin of races, sanitation laws, and how sin is responsble for changes in the universe. Christ can remove this sin and, in addition, promises a perfect world in the life to come.

REFERENCES:

The Virgin Birth and the Incarnation, by Arthur C. Custance, Ottawa, Canada. (No. 15, 1969).

Science and the Bible, by Bolton Davidheiser, Baker Book House, Grand Rapids, Mich. (1971).

Predigten und Casualreden, by C. F. W. Walther, Concordia Publishing House, St. Louis.

52. THE WELFARE LAWS OF MOSES
Deuteronomy 23:24-25

Gilbert Weaver, the author of an article in a recent issue of *Journal of the American Scientific Affiliation,* studies the religion proposed by scientists as advocated by Harlow Shapely in a book *Science Ponders Religion.* Because these people are not willing to admit their sins, they are trying to dethrone God. In His place they make a god of nature which they claim evolved without help from a higher source. Dr. Weaver describes the ethics proposed which are based solely on a relationship of man to man. The main thing in life is for people to get along in a socialistic society. These scientists criticize the Christian religion as being too much involved with God; their emphasis is on welfare programs and the like.

OLD TESTAMENT WELFARE

These critics have not read Deuteronomy 23:24-25. The poor were provided food by being permitted to eat grapes in the vineyards, but they were not allowed to gather quantities in baskets. They were also permitted to pluck ears of corn from a field, but were not allowed to use a sickle for cutting the corn. These are wholesome welfare laws providing food for the needy but avoiding waste. Heathen societies have not provided for their poor or aged, but wherever Christianity has spread, it has introduced assistance to the needy.

WELFARE RESPONSIBILITY

One of the problems with our welfare programs is that we have permitted the government to administer them with tax income. This has led to abuses, not the least of which is that concern for the needy is credited to the liberals who subscribe to the concept of evolution while denying the inerrancy of Scripture. These are not the people who have developed the basics of aiding the needy, but rather they are abusing the system so that many welfare recipients are not productive citizens. When welfare programs are administered along Christian principles, such as the Old Testament regulations on picking grapes and corn, automatic controls are provided and abuses are kept to a minimum.

Here again we see the superiority of the Christian approach over against that of the religion of science which embraces evolution.

REFERENCE:

"An Examination of a Proposed New Religion Based on Science," by Gilbert Weaver in the *Journal of the American Scientific Affiliation* (June 1968).

53. ENTROPY AND CLOTHING
Deuteronomy 29:5; 8:4

Drs. Morris and Whitcomb in *The Genesis Flood* deal at length with the scientific law of entropy. To illustrate, when a chair is burned the energy from the wood product is transformed into a gas. No energy is lost, but as it is transformed from one state to another it becomes more random, or less useful. This is the most universal of all scientific laws. These authors mention that H. F. Blum writing in *Time's Arrow and Evolution* agrees that this law argues against evolution, but in spite of this evidence, he still wants to accept evolution and therefore simply shelves the problem.

The concept of entropy is Scriptural, for we read in Psalm 102:26 that all the foundations of the earth, and all the heavens wax old like a garment. The universe is perishing. Only the eternal godhead and Scripture are immune to this universal law which has resulted from sin.

THE REVERSAL OF ENTROPY IN CLOTHING

During the forty years in which the Israelites journeyed in the wilderness, food was provided in a miraculous manner and their clothing and shoes did not wear out. Because their sandals did not wear out, they did not develop sores on their feet from much walking in the desert. This was a reversal of the law of entropy, showing that God is in control and can reverse a law when it suits His purpose. This account also establishes the concept that before sin entered the world, the law of entropy did not operate.

CHRIST AND REVERSAL

The reversal of this universal law was remarkable, yet there is an even greater reversal. Jesus Christ removed the sin which is the cause of the law, and He is able to overcome entropy. He raised Jairus' daughter from the dead, also the young man at Nain, Lazarus, and finally Himself. He arose from the dead with a renewed and glorified body. In Him we have assurance of eternal life, something which nothing in this world, not even science, can give us.

REFERENCE:

The Genesis Flood, by Morris and Whitcomb, (1961, 1971), Baker Book House, Grand Rapids, Mich.

54. THE SCIENTIFIC SEARCH FOR GOD

Deuteronomy 30:11-14; Romans 10:6-8

Dr. Oscar Leo Brauer is the author of an article "The Most Vital Question Confronting Us" included in *The Evidences of God in an Expanding Universe* edited by John C. Monsma. Dr. Brauer illustrates how man is desperately searching for the answer to origins by probing the vast reaches of space and through a study of the sun, which seemingly is a mass 330,000 times greater than the 6600 billion, billion tons of earth. Man turns to mythology, the product of imagination, to tradition which seemingly is based on the Genesis account, and to philosophy. He also turns to the physical and biological sciences and he probes the equally limitless areas inside the life cell and the atom. Still there is no satisfactory picture of origins. A great deal of time and money is wasted because much of the research is based on the assumption that life arose from inorganic material through accidental processes. Space research, particularly, is a good example of this waste. Scientists are willing to spend billions of dollars of tax money in a desperate attempt to find life in space and proofs for evolution.

SEARCH NOT NECESSARY

Author Brauer stresses that this intensive search for origins is unnecessary. From science itself we can understand that a Designer is needed to produce the design in nature. In addition, we have been given the Bible which clearly explains how the universe came to be.

In his farewell address Moses told his people thirty-five hundred years ago that it is not necessary to search for truth in the heavens or in the depths of earth. Truth is found in the open Bible, accessible to everyone who searches. Research of this record will provide an understanding of the source of origins, and scientific research will substantiate it. Moses stresses that truth, which is basic to sound scientific research, is not hidden; it is right before our eyes in Scripture. St. Paul states this forcefully in Romans 10:6-8 where he reiterates what Moses had said. The greatest of all truths, Christ's atonement for sinful man, is also clearly revealed in Scripture. If as much time were spent in Bible study as in scientific research of space, the life cell, and the atom, we would enjoy blessings beyond anything which we can imagine.

REFERENCE:

The Evidences of God in an Expanding Universe, by John C. Monsma, G. P. Putnam, N.Y. (1963).

55. BIBLE STUDY IMPROVES SCIENCE
Joshua 1:8

One of the essays in *The Challenge of Creation* published by the Bible-Science Association is "Mutations and Evolution" by Dr. Walter E. Lammerts. He notes that in 1965 agronomists at the University of California released four varieties of cherries suitable for the California climate. From their beautifully illustrated brochure he learned that this program had been started thirty-four years earlier. In contrast Lammerts had developed within five years a peach stock which did not require a somewhat cold climate in order to flower and fruit. This had been accomplished while he was also engaged with a rose breeding program.

It is the contention of Dr. Lammerts that he was able to do this superior work because he was not burdened by the evolutionary approach to the problem. His colleagues spent much time writing papers to prove evolution, which cannot be proved, and because they accepted evolution, they assumed that much time was required for a successful breeding program. With his dynamic cross-breeding approach, he accomplished more in five years than the university agronomists did in thirty-four.

PROMISE TO JOSHUA

Dr. Lammerts' success reminds us of God's promise to Joshua. Joshua was afraid to become the successor to Moses. He remembered how Aaron and Miriam had resisted Moses, how the sons of Korah had caused trouble, how the people had frequently murmured. God promised that if Joshua would meditate in His Word day and night, he would prosper and be successful. At that time Scripture consisted only of what Moses had written. Joshua steeped himself in these writings of Moses, and the Lord did indeed bless him. He became the greatest military general the

115

world has ever known. Joshua watched the Israelites cross the Jordan River on a dry bed during the spring season when its waters normally raged. He watched the walls of Jericho tumble down. He was responsible for the only forty-eight-hour day in history. In the face of great odds, his army defeated its enemies. While their enemies were mobilizing, he called for a service on Mount Ebal and Mount Gerizim, with the people shouting blessings and cursings alternately.

PROMISE TO SCIENCE

The same promise which God made to Joshua, was repeated in the Sermon on the Mount (Matthew 6:33). There Jesus tells us to seek first the kingdom of God and the blessings which we seek will be added to us. This promise applies also to science as we note in the example of Dr. Lammerts. When science is based on the Word of God, we have a superior science.

REFERENCE:

The Challenge of Creation, by Lammerts and others, Bible-Science Assn. (1964).

56. THE JORDAN WATERS PILED UP
Joshua 3:16

Velikovsky in his controversial book, *Worlds in Collision,* attempts to explain the miracles of the exodus and the conquest of Palestine by Joshua in terms of catastrophes caused by a comet which later became the planet Venus. Not wanting to admit to a miracle, he tries to explain away any divine intervention. Though he was raised as a Jew and learned the Old Testament well, he believes it is unscientific to introduce God into science.

He uses the same approach to Israel's crossing the Jordan River on dry land. It is his opinion that earth upheavals were caused by a return orbit of the comet fifty-two years after the exodus, that this produced a displacement in the earth causing the Jordan River to be dammed up by a rock slide or something similar. He contends that a slice of one bank fell on the stream, damming it sufficiently for the Israelites to cross. After the crossing, the waters chewed out this bank and the river resumed its normal course.

It is Velikovsky's claim that he has evidence according to J. Garstang in *The Foundations of Bible History,* published in 1931, that on the date of December 8, 1267, the Jordan River was dammed for sixteen hours. Following an earthquake in 1927, a slice of one bank fell into the river near the town of Adam and blocked the water flow for more than twenty-one hours.

EXPLANATIONS POSSIBLE

We do not rule out entirely explanations such as Velikovsky's. The Lord can and does make use of natural phenomena for He controls all nature, including that in space. On the other hand, such "natural" explanations are not necessary. This may have been a direct miracle which

117

cannot be explained by scientific laws, or it is possible that an earthquake dammed the Jordan River for a time.

MEANING OF NATURAL EVENTS

Here we come to an important truth. Many people try desperately to separate science and natural events from God. According to Scripture, all natural events, even catastrophes, are controlled by God, as evidenced by the Jordan River becoming a dry riverbed precisely when it was needed for the Israelites' crossing.

REFERENCE:

Worlds in Collision; by I. Velikovsky, Dell Publishing Co., N.Y. (1950).

57. THE WALLS OF JERICHO
Joshua 6:5

A handy summary of recent archaeological discoveries was compiled by H. N. Solliday in *The Bible and Archaeology*. This booklet mentions the work done in the 1930s by Professor John Garstang, financed by Sir Charles Marston. This expedition found three lines of evidence indicating that Jericho was destroyed about 1400 B.C. Pottery was found pre-dating Mycenean ware, placing the destruction prior to 1400 B.C. Also found in the ruins were scarabs (artificial beetles made from baked clay and bearing the signatures of Egyptians rulers); none could be dated later than 1400 B.C. A cemetery west of Jericho was discovered in 1932; no interments had been made later than 1400 B.C.

According to Solliday this date fits the Scriptural account of Joshua destroying Jericho by fire after her walls had tumbled down. Liberal Bible critics who contend that Jericho was destroyed in 1220 B.C. do not allow for the 300 years of the judges or the fact that Solomon began building the Temple 480 years after the Israelites left Egypt (I Kings 6:10).

VELIKOVSKY

Immanuel Velikovsky in his book *Worlds in Collision* has his own explanation of what caused the walls of Jericho to collapse. He contends that the comet's orbit which caused the earthquake which dammed up the Jordan River was also responsible for the walls of Jericho falling apart. He even claims that the sound of trumpets was not made by the priests at all, but that the sound issued from the earth, and the Israelites merely ascribed it to the priests. Velikovsky says that evidences of the walls being destroyed by an earthquake are found in the archaeological discoveries of the Garstang expedition and of an expedition by Sellin and Watzinger in 1913.

A CREATIONIST'S ATTITUDE

In the light of these claims that an earthquake was responsible for the demolition of Jericho's walls, what should be the attitude of a creationist? A Christian does not attempt to explain everything solely on the basis of natural causes but tries to find an explanation on the basis of God's direction of natural events and allows God the privilege of performing an out-and-out miracle when it suits His purpose. Velikovsky's explanation for the sound of trumpets seems to us to be directed by an unwillingness to accept anything miraculous.

Recent archaeological discoveries establishing the existence of Jericho and its destruction confirm the scientific and historical accuracy of the book of Joshua in Scripture.

SIN AND GRACE

We can also learn a lesson from the account of the fall of Jericho, and that is although God may delay His punishments, He does punish sin. Joshua is a type of Christ. As Joshua overcame Israel's enemies in Canaan, delivering the land to God's people, so Christ overcame a far greater enemy, sin, and assures us an abiding home in heaven.

REFERENCES:

The Bible and Archaeology, by H. N. Solliday, published by author at Hamburg, Iowa. (1970).

Worlds in Collision, by I. Velikovsky, Dell Publishing Co., N.Y. (1950).

58. THE FULFILLMENT OF JOSHUA'S CURSE

Joshua 6:26; I Kings 16:34

Some years ago Dr. A. W. Brustat reported on the expedition of John Garstang in the vicinity of ancient Jericho. Evidence was uncovered that the city of Jericho had been rebuilt at least four times and it was further established that the city which Joshua destroyed in 1400 B.C. had been built in 900 B.C. Traces of this city were found, including jars containing skeletons of babies, found within the foundation and gates of the city.

JOSHUA'S CURSE

Joshua pronounced a curse on anyone attempting to rebuild Jericho. He says (6:26), "Cursed be the man before the Lord, that riseth up and buildeth this city Jericho: he shall lay the foundation thereof in his firstborn, and in his youngest son shall he set up the gates of it." In I Kings 16:34 we read that in the days of Ahab's reign over Israel and Asa's rule in Judah, Hiel, the Bethelite rebuilt Jericho, and Joshua's curse was fulfilled. As Hiel laid the foundation, he lost his firstborn son, Abiram. As he set up the gates, he lost his youngest son, Segub.

Whether the jars containing skeletons of babies found in the archaeological diggings had a connection with Hiel, the builder, is hard to say. Scripture states that Joshua's curse was fulfilled, and we need no further proof from archaeology. But if archaeology confirms Scripture in this instance, it is another demonstration that the Bible is always true.

ARCHAEOLOGY CONFIRMS SCRIPTURE

In his booklet *The Bible and Archaeology*, H. N. Solliday notes that archaeology consistently confirms Scripture even when critics doubt its authority. He mentions the Rosetta Stone discovered in 1799 while Napoleon undertook his expedition through Egypt. Its hieroglyphics were deciphered and the writing was found to be much older than had been thought. It is not at all improbable that Moses wrote the first five books of the Bible at about 1440 B.C. These Egyptian hieroglyphics make mention of the Israelites. Later, in 1835, the 2700-foot-high Behistun Cliff Rock in Persia was found. Its three languages made possible the deciphering of cuneiform, from which we learned that the skill of writing and a high degree of civilization existed even prior to the Egyptian hieroglyphics. The historicity of Belshazzar was established at a time when critics denied it, claiming that Nebonidus, son and successor to Nebuchadnezzar, was reigning at that time. According to inscriptions found, Nebonidus was absent at the time and Belshazzar was substitute king during his absence. This explains why Daniel was proclaimed third ruler; Belshazzar was second ruler. Also Sargon (Isaiah 20:1) has been confirmed through archaeology, another instance where critics have been proved wrong.

It is comforting to know that true scientific research always supports the accuracy of the Bible. Because Christ is perfect, His Word also is perfect. Whenever this Word is put to the test, it comes forth as perfect and reliable.

REFERENCES:

"The Bible and Space," *by A. W. Brustat, American Lutheran Magazine* (October 1951).

The Bible and Archaeology, by H. N. Solliday, published by author at Hamburg, Iowa. (1970).

59. JOSHUA'S LONG DAY

Joshua 10:12

The *Bible-Science Newsletter* published on the front page of its April, 1970, issue an article titled "The Sun Did Stand Still," supplied by Miss Hazel Brown of Baltimore. The article concerned Harold Hill, engineer, inventor, and consultant to the space program, and a story told him by a computer operator at Greenbelt, Maryland. According to the story, space scientists were attempting to project the position of sun, moon, and stars 100 and 1,000 years from now in order to map orbits for future satellites. The computer studies revealed a day missing. This baffled the scientists until someone recalled the account of Joshua's long day. But they were still forty minutes short. That was solved when someone remembered that the sundial went backward ten degrees in the days of Hezekiah. This, they reasoned, made up the forty minutes. This story gained popularity in Christian circles. Immediately readers began checking and were told that scientists at Greenbelt knew nothing of the incident. To date Harold Hill has not provided documentation; he says only that someone did tell him of the experiment. So the conflict continues.

TOTTEN'S CALCULATIONS

Tied to this story is the work of Charles Totten, mathematician and astronomer of the past century. He made a point of the fact that Joshua commanded the sun to stand still (over Gibeon) and the moon (over Ajalon). Another translation for "stand still" is "be silent." To Totten this was proof that sun and moon were within thirteen degrees of conjunction, and he believed he had astronomical proof that this conjunction took place at the time of Joshua's battle. Totten believed that with this date established he could proceed to determine the exact week of creation.

Figuring forward from his projected creation date and backward from 1890, he found an accounting for a missing forty minutes in II Kings 20:9 at the time the sundial went backward ten degrees at Hezekiah's request. Some scientists, including Bolton Davidheiser in *News and Notes* (May 15, 1971), believe the Harold Hill story is an adaptation of Totten's work, with the computer angle added. Harry Rimmer, recognized creationist of some years ago, accepted the accuracy of Totten's figures and repeated them in his writings.

DID THE EARTH TURN OVER?

Attempts to explain how the sun could stand still in view of the concept that the earth revolves around the sun are made by Velikovsky in *Worlds in Collision* and by Howard Rand in *Joshua's Long Day*. It is their theory that a comet, preferably Venus, caused the earth to turn over, thus effecting a long day on one side of earth and a long night on the other.

THE SUN CAN STAND STILL

The command to both sun and moon to stand still or be silent agrees with the current theories that our solar system is in motion within the supposed milky way galaxy. For both sun and moon to stand still would mean that the entire solar system stood still. This does not fully explain the long day, but it offers a possible explanation in the light of current theories regarding earth's orbit around the sun.

RIDICULE

Perhaps nothing in Scripture has received as much ridicule as the account of Joshua's long day. The explanations mentioned here indicate that such a long day is not impossible and as science develops, we may find it confirmed. We need not say that Joshua is merely accommodating himself to the thinking of his day. Neither need we explain it as a refraction of the sun. This long day actually took place. As we can be sure of it, we can also be sure that sin is real and that salvation as outlined in Scripture is real.

REFERENCES:

Joshua's Long Day, by C. A. L. Totten, Destiny Publisher, Merrimac, Mass. (1890, 1968).

Worlds in Collision, by I. Velikovsky, Dell Publishing Co., N.Y. (1950).

News and Notes, by Bolton Davidheiser, published by author at La Mirada, Calif. (1971).

60. REVOLUTION OR REFORMATION?

Judges 2:10, 19

Several crusaders have been campaigning since 1963 for the removal of objectionable books from public schools in Texas. Their first and main objective was the removal of the *Biological Science Curriculum Studies* (BSCS series) because of its evolutionary content. The crusaders have also been gravely concerned with history textbooks, noting that they downgrade patriotism and present national and state heroes in an unfavorable light. A good example of this is in the high school text, *History of a Free People,* published by Macmillan, in which the authors incorrectly describe Samuel Adams as an agitator who tried to foment a revolution. Based on the evolutionary concept that progress is achieved through survival of the fittest, the modern history texts advocate socialism and revolution. Actually, encouragement of revolution and overthrow of society is a crime against the government and public schools should not be guilty of this crime.

THE EXPERIENCE OF ISRAEL

In studying Scripture's record of history, particularly that of the Israelites after Joshua's time, we note that reformation, not revolution, was needed. The generation which had conquered Palestine under Joshua remained faithful to the Lord. The next generation, and particularly the following one, turned from God to worship the idols of Baal and Ashtaroth. For these sins God punished them. In their afflictions they turned again to the Lord and He sent them deliverers known as the judges, among whom were Gideon, Deborah and Samson. By the third generation the people had again forsaken the Lord. When God punished them again, they called to Him for help. He sent another deliverer and they reformed for a time. The history of Israel points up the need for reformation. There was revolution, but it was always a sign of degradation and of anarchy, never an improvement of society or a blessing.

SIN AND GRACE

This is a picture of a Christian's everyday life. Every day Christians should exercise respect for authority and should encourage reformation, recognizing the impact of sin and the desperate need for a Savior from sin.

REFERENCE:

High School Biology Textbook Controversy, by Mr. and Mrs. Mel Gabler, published by authors at Longview, Texas. (1966).